Revise

Pearson Edexcel GCSE
Spanish
Revision Workbook

Author: Viv Halksworth
Series consultant: Harry Smith

Audio for Speaking and Listening at your fingertips

Scan the green audio QR codes to immediately launch high-quality recordings of native speakers. These are exam-style tracks for realistic assessment practice and can particularly help you with:

Listen to the recording

- **Listening: Dictation task practice**
  Listen three times for exam-style practice.
- **Speaking: Read aloud practice**
  Targeted pronunciation practice of sounds helps build your confidence.
- **Speaking: Role play practice**
  Hear the teacher part and speak your answers in the pauses.

Transcripts for all audio files can be accessed here.

Transcripts

Support for longer writing tasks

Space is provided in this Workbook but sometimes you'll need to use your own paper too. Full sample student responses are given in the answer section so that you can self-assess. Remember that there is more than one correct answer for this type of question.

Practice papers

Help to check that you are exam-ready with a full set of practice papers containing exam-style questions for Speaking, Listening, Reading and Writing, for both Foundation and Higher tier.

Higher and Foundation tiers

Questions which only apply to Higher Tier are marked with an

Difficulty scale

The icon next to each exam-style question tells you how difficult it is.

Some questions cover a range of difficulties.

Target grade 4

Target grade 7-8

Also available:

The Revision Guide helps you revise vocabulary and grammar with a manageable topic-by-topic approach. Worked example questions and pages on each exam paper will build your skills ready for assessment, and digital resources such as quick quizzes, vocab checks, videos and flashcards are all included!

Pearson Edexcel publishes the only official Sample Assessment Material on its website. The questions in this Workbook have been designed to familiarise you with the type of tasks you may meet in the exam, and are tailored to help you to practise specific skills. Remember that the actual assessments may not look like this.

Contents

My people
1 Introducing yourself
2 Physical descriptions
3 Character descriptions
4 Family
5 What makes a good friend
6 Relationships (family and friends)
7 Helping a friend
8 Everyday life
9 Meals at home
10 Celebrations

Health
11 Food and drink
12 Healthy diets
13 Sport and exercise
14 Physical wellbeing
15 Mental wellbeing
16 Feeling unwell
17 Role models in sport
18 Sporting events

Media and technology
19 Me and my mobile
20 Social media
21 The internet
22 Computer games
23 The good and bad of technology

Free time
24 Hobbies
25 Music and dance
26 Music and dance events
27 Reading
28 Television
29 The cinema
30 What's the story?
31 Celebrities and role models

Local environment and transport
32 Places in town
33 Things to do in town
34 Shopping for clothes
35 Transport
36 Travel on public transport and buying tickets
37 My region – good and bad
38 My region in the past
39 Town or country?

Tourism
40 Plans for the holidays
41 Holiday preferences
42 Types of holidays
43 Where to stay
44 Booking accommodation
45 Holiday activities
46 Trips and visits
47 Giving or asking for directions
48 Shopping for gifts
49 Tourist information
50 Tourist attractions
51 Holiday problems
52 Accommodation problems
53 Eating out
54 Opinions about food
55 The weather
56 Customs and festivals
57 A visit to Barcelona
58 A visit to Buenos Aires

My school
59 School subjects
60 School subjects – likes and dislikes
61 The school day
62 School facilities
63 School uniform
64 Activities in class
65 School rules
66 School – the good and the bad
67 School clubs and activities
68 Being a good student

My future
69 Options at 16
70 Equality
71 Future study plans
72 Future plans
73 Part-time jobs and money
74 Opinions about jobs
75 Pros and cons of different jobs
76 Job adverts, skills needed
77 Applying for jobs
78 Preparing for interviews
79 Working to help others
80 Equality and helping others

Environment
81 The environment and me
82 Local environmental issues
83 Global environmental issues
84 Caring for the planet
85 A greener future

About the exams
86 Practice for Paper 1: Speaking
87 Practice for Paper 1: Speaking
88 Practice for Paper 2: Listening
89 Practice for Paper 2: Listening
90 Practice for Paper 3: Reading
91 Practice for Paper 3: Reading
92 Practice for Paper 4: Writing
93 Practice for Paper 4: Writing

Grammar
94 Nouns and articles
95 Adjectives
96 Possessives and pronouns
97 Comparisons
98 Other adjectives
99 Pronouns
100 The present tense
101 Reflexive verbs
102 Irregular verbs (present)
103 *Ser* and *estar*
104 The gerund / present participle
105 The preterite tense
106 The imperfect tense
107 The future tense
108 The conditional tense
109 The perfect tense
110 Giving instructions
111 The present subjunctive
112 Negatives
113 Special verbs
114 *Por* and *para*
115 Asking questions
116 The passive
117 Numbers

Practice papers
118 Paper 1: Speaking (Foundation)
119 Paper 2: Listening (Foundation)
122 Paper 3: Reading (Foundation)
127 Paper 4: Writing (Foundation)
129 Paper 1: Speaking (Higher)
131 Paper 2: Listening (Higher)
134 Paper 3: Reading (Higher)
139 Paper 4: Writing (Higher)

141 Answers

A small bit of small print
Pearson Edexcel publishes Sample Assessment Material and the Specification on its website. This is the official content and this book should be used in conjunction with it. The questions in this Workbook have been written to help you practise every topic in the book. Remember: the real exam questions may not look like this.

1-to-1 page match with the Spanish Revision Guide
ISBN 9781292739687

Had a go ☐   Nearly there ☐   Nailed it! ☐

My people

Introducing yourself

A message from a new Spanish friend

1 Read this text message.

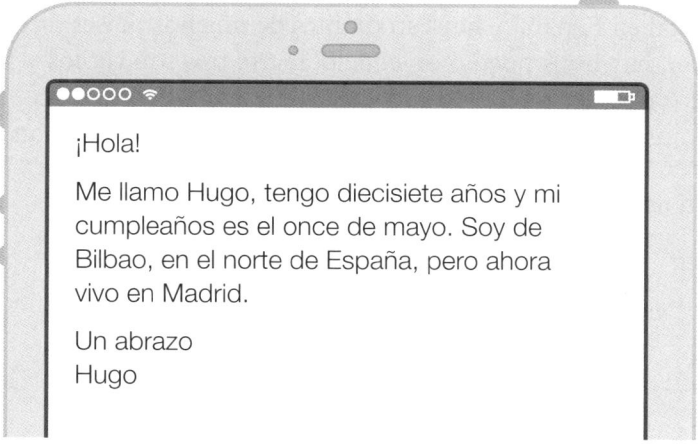

> ¡Hola!
>
> Me llamo Hugo, tengo diecisiete años y mi cumpleaños es el once de mayo. Soy de Bilbao, en el norte de España, pero ahora vivo en Madrid.
>
> Un abrazo
> Hugo

> Be careful not to confuse numbers. Make sure you know the difference between *dieciséis* (sixteen) and *diecisiete* (seventeen).
>
> Also, don't be misled by the word *once*, which means 'eleven' (and has nothing to do with the word 'one'!).

Put a cross [×] in each of the **three** correct boxes.

Hugo …

☐	**A** is sixteen.
☐	**B** will be eighteen in May.
☐	**C** was born on 1 May.
☐	**D** is from Bilbao.
☐	**E** comes from northern Spain.
☐	**F** used to live in Madrid.

(3 marks)

Birthdays

2 Manuel, Nadia and Jorge are talking about themselves.

What do they say?

Complete the gap in each sentence using a word from the box below. There are more words than gaps.

> spring   summer   autumn   winter
> north   south   east

(a) Manuel's birthday is in .... (1 mark)

(b) Nadia lives in the .... (1 mark)

(c) Jorge was born in .... (1 mark)

1

My people

Had a go ☐ Nearly there ☐ Nailed it! ☐

Physical descriptions

In my class

1 Read Natalia's account of the students in her class.

> Voy a un instituto internacional en España y hay estudiantes de muchos países diferentes. Muchos tienen el pelo marrón, hay unos pocos con el pelo negro, tres son rubios y solo hay una chica pelirroja. Los chicos que tienen el pelo rubio tienen los ojos azules o grises. La chica del pelo rojo tiene los ojos verdes y muy bonitos. Hay siete en total que llevan gafas.

Complete the gap in each sentence using a word from the box below.

black	brown	red	fair
green	grey	blue	
three	six	seven	eight

(a) Most students have .... hair.

(b) There are .... fair-haired students.

(c) Only one student has .... hair.

(d) The students with fair hair have blue or .... eyes.

(e) A total of .... students wear glasses.

(5 marks)

Appearances

2 These people are talking about the aspects of their appearance that they like and dislike.

What do they say?

Listen to the recording and complete the following table **in English**.

You do not need to write in full sentences.

	Likes	**Dislikes**
(a)		
(b)		
(c)		
(d)		

(8 marks)

> You won't always hear the verb *gustar* when people are talking about their likes and dislikes. They could use other ways to express their preferences including *me encanta(n)*, or verbs like *odiar*.

Had a go ☐ Nearly there ☐ Nailed it! ☐

My people

Character descriptions

A new TV programme

1 Read this description of a new Spanish children's TV programme.

Una nueva serie de televisión
El martes empieza una nueva serie sobre las aventuras de cuatro chicos y su perro. Luis, el chico mayor, es serio y responsable y le gusta ser el jefe del grupo. La chica mayor se llama Marta y es muy deportista. Al final del día siempre está un poco cansada porque hace mucho ejercicio. Luego está Nadim, un chico simpático y tranquilo, muy popular con los otros porque siempre está contento de ayudarlos. La más joven se llama Sara, una chica alegre y divertida con una actitud positiva.

See this photo in colour

Which character matches these descriptions? Put a cross [×] in the correct column for each question.

	Who …	Luis	Marta	Nadim	Sara	
(a)	… is the most helpful?					(1 mark)
(b)	… is the youngest?					(1 mark)
(c)	… always gets tired?					(1 mark)
(d)	… is the natural leader?					(1 mark)
(e)	… has a positive outlook?					(1 mark)
(f)	… is the sporty one?					(1 mark)

Translation

2 Translate the paragraph **into Spanish**. (well → *bueno / pues*)

> What is my personality like? Well, I think that I am friendly and fun, with a positive and optimistic attitude. I am quite hard-working and responsible. I am not very sporty, but I am cheerful. My friends say that I am clever, but I am nervous when I have exams.

> Be careful with word order in the second sentence. In the phrase 'with a positive and optimistic attitude' the noun 'attitude' needs to come first in Spanish, followed by the two adjectives. (→ 'an attitude positive and optimistic')

....
....
....
....
....
.... **(10 marks)**

3

My people   Had a go ☐   Nearly there ☐   Nailed it! ☐

Family

Paula's family

1 Read Paula's email about her family.

> ✉
> ¡Hola!
> Antes de visitarnos en abril, necesitas saber un poco sobre la familia con quien vas a vivir. Mis padres, Sebastián y Rosalía, son de un pueblo en el sur de Argentina, pero viven aquí en Málaga desde hace casi veinte años. Tengo un hermano menor, Marcos, que es irritante y muy activo. Mi hermana mayor se llama Sofía. Es alta y bonita con el pelo largo y negro y los ojos grandes y azules. Desafortunadamente, ¡no me parezco nada a ella! Sofía tiene veintidós años y vive con su pareja en el centro de la ciudad. Mis abuelos viven en una casa muy cerca con nuestra tía Elena, que nunca se casó.
> Un abrazo
> Paula

Put a cross [×] in each one of the **three** correct boxes.

☐	A	Paula's parents come from northern Argentina.
☐	B	They moved to Málaga nearly 20 years ago.
☐	C	Marcos is annoying.
☐	D	Paula looks a lot like her sister.
☐	E	Sofía got married when she was 22.
☐	F	Paula's aunt Elena is not married.

> Each of the statements in the answer options grid contains a key word that is your starting point when searching for the answer in the text. Start with Argentina, Málaga, Marcos, sister, 22 and Elena, and read around the word to find the answer.

(3 marks)

A family photo

See this photo in colour

2 Describe this picture.

Your description **must** cover:
- people
- location
- activity.

(8 marks)

Listen to the recording

When you have finished your description, listen to the recording of two further questions on the same topic. Pause the recording to give your answers.

(4 marks)

There is a sample recording in the Answers section to give you more ideas.

Had a go ☐ Nearly there ☐ Nailed it! ☐

My people

What makes a good friend

Read aloud

1 Sara writes about her best friend.

Read out the text below.

> Mi mejor amiga siempre está ahí cuando la necesito.
> Es simpática y tenemos mucho en común. Me escucha y me acepta, pero no le importa decirme la verdad.
> Compartimos los mismos intereses en música y vamos a conciertos juntas.
> Es una chica graciosa que me hace reír todo el tiempo.

You can check your reading by listening to a recording of the text in the Answers section. You can also hear sample answers to the questions.

> When *c* is followed by *a*, *o* or *u*, it has a sound like 'k' in 'kiss' (mú**ca**, **co**mún, es**cu**cha).
> When it is followed by *e* or *i* it has a sound like 'th' in 'thin' (gra**ci**osa, ne**ce**sito).
> If 'c' is followed by 'u' and another vowel, it forms a sound like 'kw' (**cu**ando).
> The letters *ch* in Spanish are like the English 'ch' in 'chat'.

Once you have read the text aloud, listen to the two recorded questions related to what you have read. Pause the recording after each one to give yourself time to answer.

You are expected to say a few words or a short phrase / sentence in response to each question. One-word answers will not be enough to gain full marks.

(12 marks)

> After you have read the passage in the exam, you will hand the card back to your teacher, so you won't be able to use the vocabulary from the card. However, the questions will be on the same topic and they will ask (1) about something you like doing and (2) your opinion of something.

Translation

2 Translate the following sentences **into English**.

(a) Mi mejor amiga me ayuda mucho.

....

(b) Me gusta pensar que soy un buen amigo.

....

(c) Un amigo perfecto siempre te acepta como eres.

....

 (d) La amistad es muy importante para los jóvenes.

....

(e) Hay momentos cuando tu amigo necesita decirte la verdad.

....

(10 marks)

5

My people

Had a go ☐ Nearly there ☐ Nailed it! ☐

Relationships (family and friends)

Family relationships

1 Read these comments from an internet forum.

> **Luisa:** Cuando era pequeña, me peleaba mucho con mi hermana mayor. Pero cuando empecé a ir al instituto, ella me cuidaba y me defendía de las chicas mayores que no eran muy simpáticas.
>
> **Amira:** Estoy muy enfadada con mis padres porque a mi hermano y a mí nos tratan diferente. Él tiene mucha más libertad que yo y, en mi opinión, esto no es justo. Deberían tratarnos con igualdad.
>
> **Diego:** Tengo que compartir dormitorio con mi hermano menor y me molesta mucho. Siempre hace ruido cuando intento estudiar y terminamos discutiendo todo el tiempo. Necesito mi propio espacio.

Who says what? Choose the correct answers.

Put a cross [×] in the correct column for each question.

	Who …	Luisa	Amira	Diego
(a)	… wants more freedom?			
(b)	… needs their own space?			
(c)	… used to fight a lot?			
(d)	… is always arguing?			
(e)	… was protected at school?			
(f)	… thinks their parents are unfair?			

(6 marks)

A letter about friends

2 Write a letter to your friend about friends.

You **must** include the following points:
- how well you get on with your friends
- the reasons for any arguments
- what you and your friends will do this weekend.

Write your answer **in Spanish**. You should aim to write between 40 and 50 words.

> Don't think that you need to write lots to score good marks. Stick to the word count recommendation and aim for quality, not quantity.

....
....
....
....
....

(14 marks)

Had a go ☐ **Nearly there** ☐ **Nailed it!** ☐   My people

Helping a friend

Dictation

1 You are going to hear someone talking about friends.

Sentences 1–2: write down the missing words in the gaps provided. In each gap, you will write one word **in Spanish**.

Example: *Creo que los amigos son muy importantes.*

1 Mi .... amigo .... me ....

2 Mis .... de .... me ....

Sentences 3–6: write down the full sentences that you hear in the spaces provided, **in Spanish**.

Example: *Mi mejor amiga y yo hacemos juntas la tarea.*

3 ....
4 ....
5 ....
6 .... **(10 marks)**

> Remember that you hear each sentence three times. Make sure your writing is really clear and, if you want to change a word, put a clear line through it and write the new word above.

Picture card

See this photo in colour

2 Describe this picture.

Your description **must** cover:
- people
- location
- activity.

> During the 15-minute preparation time before the Speaking exam, take a moment or two to consider what the two questions relating to the photo might be about. For example, here you know the photo is about friends so you could jot down a couple of ideas or connected vocabulary.

When you have finished your description, play the recording to hear two questions relating to the picture. Pause after each question to give yourself time to answer. You are expected to say a few words or a short phrase / sentence in response to each question. One-word answers will not be sufficient to gain full marks.

You can hear a sample description and sample answers in the Answers section.

My people

Had a go ☐   Nearly there ☐   Nailed it! ☐

Everyday life

Family life

1 Miguel, Ana and David are talking about their daily routines.

What do they say?

Listen to the recording and complete the sentences by putting a cross [×] in the correct box for each question.

(a) During the week Miguel gets up at …

☐	A	nine o'clock.
☐	B	seven o'clock.
☐	C	eight o'clock.

> Remember that you have five minutes to read through the Listening paper questions before the recording starts. Always pay attention to the question titles, which tell you what topic each question is about.

(1 mark)

(b) Ana says that, in her family, …

☐	A	they often have afternoon naps.
☐	B	no one has time for a siesta.
☐	C	only her grandmother has an afternoon nap.

(1 mark)

(c) David says …

☐	A	he doesn't have breakfast.
☐	B	he has a sandwich for breakfast.
☐	C	he buys something to eat at school.

(1 mark)

Translation

2 Translate the following five sentences **into Spanish**.

(a) I eat my breakfast in the kitchen.

....

(b) Normally I get up at eight o'clock.

....

(c) He leaves the house and catches the bus.

....

(d) I do my homework after the evening meal.

....

(e) Last weekend I watched television with my family.

....

(10 marks)

> Always have a go at as much of the translation as possible. If there are words you don't know, don't abandon the whole sentence, as you will get marks for all the sections that you can do.

Had a go ☐ Nearly there ☐ Nailed it! ☐

My people

Meals at home

Eating at home

1 Read Sara's blog about typical meals at home.

> Normalmente tomamos el desayuno a horas diferentes en mi casa porque todos tenemos un horario distinto. Yo no tomo mucho: algo de fruta y un café con mucha leche. Durante la semana comemos sobre las tres. Mi abuela prepara la comida porque mis padres trabajan. Sin embargo, todos volvemos a casa para comer y hablamos de nuestro día. A veces es un poco difícil porque mi hermana menor es muy irritante y se niega a comer las verduras. La cena es una comida más ligera, y la tomamos sobre las nueve.

What does Sara tell us? Answer the questions **in English**. You do not need to write in full sentences.

(a) What time do they all have breakfast?

.... **(1 mark)**

(b) Who prepares lunch?

.... **(1 mark)**

(c) Why does Sara say her sister is annoying?

.... **(1 mark)**

(d) How does Sara describe the evening meal?

.... **(1 mark)**

> The text refers to three different people, so you have to find out which one of the three prepares the lunch to answer question (b).

Translation

2 Translate the following five sentences **into English**.

(a) Tomo una merienda cuando vuelvo del instituto.

....

(b) Llevo un bocadillo al colegio para comer durante el recreo.

....

(c) Ayer cenamos sobre las diez.

....

(d) Este domingo vamos a preparar la comida para mis abuelos.

....

(e) Los fines de semana me gusta ayudar a cocinar.

....

> With the translation into English task, in the exam you will have a title that tells you the topic of all of the sentences. Here, the topic is at the top of the page. Always bear this in mind so that if there is any vocabulary you don't know, at least you can make a sensible guess.

(10 marks)

My people

Had a go ☐ Nearly there ☐ Nailed it! ☐

Celebrations

Dictation

1 You are going to hear someone talking about special occasions.

Sentences 1–3: write down the missing words in the gaps provided. In each gap, you will write one word **in Spanish**.

Example: Vamos a <u>hacer</u> un <u>pastel</u>.

1 .... una fiesta de ....

2 .... en un ....

3 Voy a .... muchas ....

Sentences 4–6: write down the full sentences that you hear in the spaces provided, **in Spanish**.

Example: <u>Bailamos toda la noche</u>.

4 ....

5 ....

6 ....

> Remember that the letter *h* is silent in Spanish. The verb *hacer*, in all tenses, begins with a silent *h*. For example, *hice* (I did / made), *haré* (I will do / make) and *hago* (I do / make). Listen out for one of these in the dictation.

(10 marks)

Picture task

See this photo in colour

2 Describe the photo. Write four short sentences **in Spanish**.

.... **(2 marks)**

.... **(2 marks)**

.... **(2 marks)**

.... **(2 marks)**

> It's a really good idea to study the present continuous tense so you can say what people **are doing** in the photo. It is not a difficult tense to learn: *estoy / estás / está / estamos / estáis / están* + *-ando* (for *-ar* verbs) or *-iendo* (for *-er* and *-ir* verbs). For example, *están celebrando* – they are celebrating; *está abriendo* – he is opening.

Had a go ☐ Nearly there ☐ Nailed it! ☐

Health

Food and drink

Eating out

1 Read these reviews of a restaurant.

> **Nadia:** Decidimos no tomar entrantes, lo que fue una buena decisión porque la paella que compartimos era enorme. Estaba muy rica y el arroz fue cocinado perfectamente. De postre, mi marido tomó un pastel de naranja, pero yo no pude comer más.
>
> **Emilio:** Vamos a este restaurante a menudo porque soy alérgico al pescado y la calidad de la carne allí es excelente. Anoche la cena fue tan buena como siempre y el servicio rápido, aunque pienso que los precios han subido bastante recientemente.
>
> **Carmen:** Ayer mi familia y yo disfrutamos de una tarde muy agradable en el restaurante, probando las muchas tapas que hay. Lo que me gusta más es que preparan el tipo de comida que prefiero – típicamente española y tradicional.

Complete the sentences below. Put a cross [×] in the correct box for each question.

(a) Nadia thought the *paella* was …

☐	**A** disappointing.
☐	**B** huge.
☐	**C** under-cooked.

(b) Nadia …

☐	**A** had an orange cake for pudding.
☐	**B** had fruit for dessert.
☐	**C** did not have dessert.

(c) Emilio likes the restaurant because of …

☐	**A** the quality of the fish.
☐	**B** how good the meat is.
☐	**C** the freshness of the seafood.

(d) Carmen's favourite type of food is …

☐	**A** a mixture of international cuisine.
☐	**B** different dishes of tapas.
☐	**C** traditional Spanish cooking.

(4 marks)

An email

2 Write an email to your friend about food.

You **must** include the following points:

- what you like to eat
- a meal you had recently
- your opinion of the meal with reasons
- what you are going to make for a special occasion in the future.

Write your answer **in Spanish**. You should aim to write between 80 and 90 words.

> Remember the rules about using *gustar*: use *gusta* if what follows is singular, or a verb, and *gustan* if what follows is plural. Also remember to include the article (*el, la, los, las*) with nouns after *gustar*.

....
....
....
....
....
....
....

(18 marks)

Health

Had a go ☐ Nearly there ☐ Nailed it! ☐

Healthy diets

Picture task

See this photo in colour

1 Describe this picture. Your description **must** cover:
- people
- location
- activity.

When you have finished your description, play the recording and answer the two questions relating to the picture. You are expected to say a few words or a short phrase / sentence in response to each question. One-word answers will not be sufficient to gain full marks.

(12 marks)

Listen to the recording

> Remember that you can use words that are not on the prescribed vocabulary list in either the Speaking or the Writing exam. You can use any of the vocabulary that you know. Here it would be useful to remember the word *ensalada* for 'salad'.

Read aloud

2 Daniel, your Chilean friend, tells you about his eating habits. Read out the text below.

> Normalmente tomo un huevo y un poco de pan para el desayuno. Evito la comida rápida como las hamburguesas, pero me gusta tomar un bocadillo de queso para el almuerzo. También me encantan los churros y el chocolate.

Listen to the recording

Once you have read the text, play the recording and answer the two questions related to what you have read.

You are expected to say a few words or a short phrase / sentence in response to each question. One-word answers will not be sufficient to gain full marks.

(12 marks)

You can hear a recording of the text and sample answers in the Answers section.

> Remember that the *u* in *queso* is not pronounced, so the sound is like 'kay' and not 'kway'. Double *ll* (as in *bocadillo*) can be pronounced like the 'li' in 'mi<u>ll</u>ion' or the 'y' in '<u>y</u>ellow'.

Had a go ☐ Nearly there ☐ Nailed it! ☐   **Health**

Sport and exercise

Getting fit

1 Lucía, Mario and Sara are talking about exercise.

What do they say?

Listen to the recording and complete the following table **in English**. You do not need to write in full sentences.

> Listen out for words like *bueno, mejor, ventaja* for the positive aspects and words like *malo, peor, desventaja* for the negative aspects.

(a) Lucía (swimming)

Advantage	....
Disadvantage	....

(2 marks)

(b) Mario (cycling)

Advantage	....
Disadvantage	....

(2 marks)

(c) Sara (basketball)

Advantage	....
Disadvantage	....

(2 marks)

Role play

2 **Setting: At the sports centre**

Scenario:
- You are at a sports centre, booking tickets to see a basketball match.
- Play the recording to hear the teacher's role.
- You will hear questions **in Spanish** and you must answer **in Spanish** in the pauses.
- You are expected to say a few words or a short phrase / sentence in response to each prompt. One-word answers will not be sufficient to gain full marks.

> **Task:**
> 1 Say what tickets you want.
> 2 Say what day the match is.
> 3 Say how many tickets you want.
> 4 Give your opinion about the sport.
> 5 Ask a question about the price.

> Remember that tickets for an event are *entradas* and tickets for travel are *billetes*.

(10 marks)

Health

Had a go ☐   Nearly there ☐   Nailed it! ☐

Physical wellbeing

Picture task

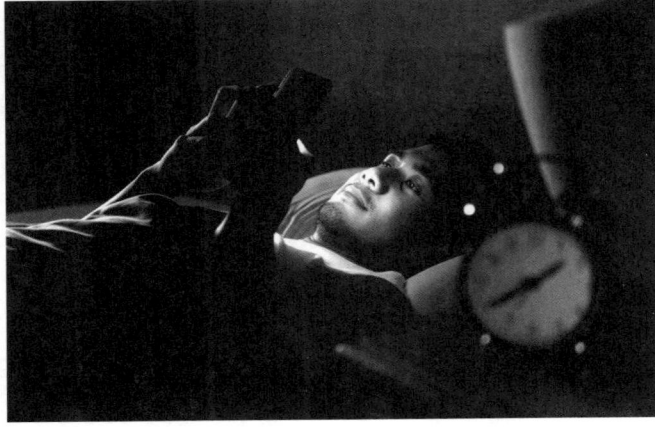

See this photo in colour

1 Describe this picture.

Your description **must** cover:
- people
- location
- activity.

Listen to the recording

When you have finished your description, play the recording and answer the two questions relating to the picture. You are expected to say a few words or a short phrase / sentence in response to each question. One-word answers will not be sufficient to gain full marks.

(12 marks)

Translation

2 Translate the following sentences **into Spanish**.

(a) My brother sleeps very well every night.

....

(b) I like to spend time in the open air.

....

(c) I drank lots of water yesterday.

....

(d) The sun can do damage to your skin.

....

(e) She is very tired today.

....

(10 marks)

Had a go ☐   Nearly there ☐   Nailed it! ☐

Health

Mental wellbeing

Looking after your mental wellbeing

1 David, Alba and Luis are talking about mental wellbeing.

What do they say?

Listen to the recording and complete the sentences by putting a cross [×] in the correct box for each question.

(a) David thinks you shouldn't spend all your time …

☐	A on school work.
☐	B worrying.
☐	C relaxing.

(b) He unwinds by …

☐	A playing sport.
☐	B going out with friends.
☐	C watching a match.

(c) In the past, at school, Alba felt …

☐	A bullied.
☐	B she was failing.
☐	C ill with stress.

(d) Alba's sister helps …

☐	A with Alba's homework.
☐	B by listening.
☐	C because she gives good advice.

(e) Luis says he …

☐	A never gets upset.
☐	B very often gets anxious.
☐	C is occasionally sad.

(f) He lets out his emotions …

☐	A when he sings on stage.
☐	B in the lyrics he writes.
☐	C through listening to music.

(6 marks)

> The alternative options in multiple choice questions often use vocabulary that you will hear in the recording. This means that you are listening for detail and not the general gist. Careful listening will allow you to reject the wrong answers and arrive at the correct one.

Translation

2 Translate the following sentences **into English**.

(a) Me gusta pintar porque es muy relajante.

....

(b) Mi abuelo siempre me escucha si tengo un problema.

....

(c) Cuando me siento triste, hablo con mis amigos.

....

(d) Ayudé a mi hermano cuando tenía un problema.

....

(e) Las relaciones familiares son muy importantes para la salud mental.

....

(10 marks)

> The *me* in sentence (b) needs to be translated; it is the object of the verb for which *abuelo* is the subject. However, the *me* in sentence (c) does not need to be put into English because *sentirse* is a reflexive verb in Spanish, but 'to feel' is not reflexive in English.

Health

Had a go ☐   Nearly there ☐   Nailed it! ☐

Feeling unwell

Role play

1 **Setting: At the doctor's**

  Scenario:
  - You are at the doctor's.
  - Play the recording to hear the teacher's role.
  - You will hear questions **in Spanish** and you must answer **in Spanish** in the pauses.
  - You are expected to say a few words or a short phrase / sentence in response to each prompt. One-word answers will not be sufficient to gain full marks.

  Task:
  1 Tell the doctor what the problem is.
  2 Say what caused the problem.
  3 Say how long you are going to be in Spain.
  4 Say what day you will be returning home.
  5 Ask a question about the pharmacy opening hours.

> When talking about what caused your problem (task 2), you could use the past continuous (*estar* in the imperfect tense followed by the present participle *-ando / -iendo*):
>
> Examples: *Estaba paseando en bicicleta cuando me caí.* – I was going for a bike ride when I fell.
>
> *Estaba tomando el sol y me quemé.* – I was sunbathing and I got burnt.
>
> *Estaba jugando al vóleibol en la playa cuando me corté.* – I was playing volleyball on the beach when I cut myself.

(10 marks)

An article

2 Write an article about an accident you had while on holiday.

  You **must** include the following points:
  - what you were doing at the time
  - the type of injury
  - what you did next.

  Write your answer **in Spanish**. You should aim to write between 40 and 50 words.

....
....
....
....
....
....
....
....
....
....
....
....

(14 marks)

Had a go ☐ Nearly there ☐ Nailed it! ☐   Health

Role models in sport

Changes in sport

1 Read this article about women's football and answer the following questions **in English**.

> En 2022 vimos el primer partido de fútbol masculino* en una Copa del Mundo con una mujer, Stéphanie Frappart, como árbitra**. Estaba muy contenta cuando vi este partido porque además de tener una mujer como árbitra, también había dos mujeres como juezas de línea*** – una **brasileña** y una mexicana. Cuando yo era joven, las chicas simplemente no jugaban al fútbol, no estaba permitido. Solo nos dejaban jugar al tenis o hacer atletismo ¡pero nunca con los chicos! Cada día hay más igualdad en el deporte, pero todavía hay mucho por hacer.

*fútbol masculino – men's football
**árbitra – female referee
***jueza de línea – line judge, assistant referee

(a) Why did Stéphanie Frappart make the headlines in 2022?

....

(b) What else was remarkable about the match?

....

(c) Which of these is the best translation for the word **brasileña**? Put a cross [×] in the correct box.

☐	A	from Barcelona
☐	B	Brazilian
☐	C	left back

(d) What does the writer say about football for girls when she was young?

....

(e) What does she say about equality in sport in the modern day? Put a cross [×] in the correct box.

☐	A	She is delighted at the progress made.
☐	B	She thinks there is still some way to go.
☐	C	She is disappointed at the lack of change.

(5 marks)

Translation

2 Translate the paragraph **into Spanish**.

> My name is Paula and this year I am the captain of the football team in my school. I love sport because it helps me to keep fit and I enjoy the friendship with the team members. Last week we won the match but this Saturday I think we will lose against a very good team.

| Notice that the writer is female. Therefore, you will need the feminine word for 'captain'. |

....
....
....
....

(10 marks)

17

Health

Had a go ☐ Nearly there ☐ Nailed it! ☐

Sporting events

Sporting events

1 Read three social media comments about sporting events.

> **Sara:** La semana pasada fui con mi familia a ver un partido de fútbol en el estadio de la ciudad. Desafortunadamente, no nos divertimos porque estaba lloviendo y tuvimos bastante frío.
>
> **Vicente:** Anoche mi prima jugó en un partido de baloncesto en silla de ruedas en el centro de deportes. Había mucha gente allí y tuvimos una experiencia maravillosa porque el ambiente fue muy emocionante.
>
> **Lola:** Ayer mi hermano participó en unas carreras de monopatinaje y fuimos al estadio para ver la competición. Pasamos una tarde agradable porque mi hermano ganó varias carreras.

What do Sara, Vicente and Lola say about the events?

Complete the tables **in English**. You do not need to write in full sentences.

(a) Sara

Opinion of the event	....
Reason	....

(2 marks)

(b) Vicente

Opinion of the event	....
Reason	....

(2 marks)

(c) Lola

Opinion of the event	....
Reason	....

(2 marks)

Picture task

2 Describe this picture.

Your description **must** cover:
- people
- location
- activity.

See this photo in colour

When you have finished your description, play the recording to hear and answer two questions relating to the picture. You are expected to say a few words or a short phrase / sentence in response to each question. One-word answers will not be sufficient to gain full marks.

(12 marks)

Had a go ☐ **Nearly there** ☐ **Nailed it!** ☐

Media and technology

Me and my mobile

Picture task

1   Describe the photo. Write four short sentences **in Spanish**.

    .... **(2 marks)**
    .... **(2 marks)**
    .... **(2 marks)**
    .... **(2 marks)**

> You only need the present tense in this question on the Foundation Writing paper but, if verbs are not your strong point, learn *hay* (there is / there are), *tiene* (he / she has), *tienen* (they have), *está en* (he / she is in) and *están en* (they are in). These will allow you to say a variety of things.

Dictation

2   You are going to hear someone talking about mobile phones.

Sentences 1–3: write down the missing words in the gaps provided. In each gap, you will write one word **in Spanish**.

Example: *Uso mi <u>móvil</u> todo el <u>tiempo</u>.*

1 Esta .... es muy ....

2 Los .... son bastante ....

3 Vas a .... la ....

Sentences 4–6: write down the full sentences that you hear in the spaces provided, **in Spanish**.

Example: <u>*Me gusta buscar información en internet.*</u>

4 ....
5 ....
6 .... **(10 marks)**

Media and technology

Had a go ☐   Nearly there ☐   Nailed it! ☐

Social media

Listen to the recording

A conversation about social networks

1 Marco, Amira, Javier and Sofía are talking about social networks.

What do they say?

Complete the gap in each sentence using a word or phrase from the box below.

There are more words / phrases than gaps.

> Pay close attention to the wording of each question. Not all the answers fit grammatically in all the questions so you can rule these out straight away. For example, sentences (a) and (b) can only be followed by the phrases on the top line of the box. In general, work your way down the word cloud in order as you answer questions (a) to (e).

> find old friends   meet new people   pass the time   find a partner
> the issue of security online   the false information   the fun things
> the lack of parental control   the problem of fraud
> the privacy issues   the hurtful comments

(a) Marco thinks social media help you to ....

(b) Amira says they helped her ....

(c) Javier points out ....

(d) Sofía is saddened by ....

(e) Sofía is worried about ....

(5 marks)

Read aloud

2 Raúl, your Mexican friend, tells you about social media.

Read out the text below.

> Es muy importante no publicar información en tu página que debería ser privada. Dicen que algunos jefes miran las redes sociales antes de darte un trabajo. Recomiendan no compartir tus datos personales porque alguien podría robarlos.

> You can make notes on the card that contains the Read aloud task. Try to work out the meaning of the text during the preparation task, and put a little ^ sign where you think there is a slight natural pause in the sentence. For instance, in the final sentence, you could put a ^ sign between *personales* and *porque*. The sentence means 'They recommend not sharing your personal details ... because someone could steal them'. If you recognise the meaning of the passage, it will sound better when you read it aloud.

To check your pronunciation, you can hear a recording of the text in the Answers section.

Had a go ☐ Nearly there ☐ Nailed it! ☐   **Media and technology**

The internet

The internet

1 David, Ana and Miguel are talking about the internet.

What do they say?

Listen to the recording and complete the sentences by putting a cross [×] in the correct box for each question.

(a) David thinks that …

☐	**A** the internet is brilliant for studying.
☐	**B** the information is not always accurate.
☐	**C** people are not who they say they are.

(1 mark)

(b) Ana says that …

☐	**A** the internet is really fast in her house.
☐	**B** there is too much information out there.
☐	**C** it's not hard to work out what is true.

(1 mark)

(c) Miguel says that using the internet means that …

☐	**A** homework takes him even longer.
☐	**B** he spends too much time playing games online.
☐	**C** he saves time doing his schoolwork.

(1 mark)

My mother's hobby

1 Read Sara's article about her mother's hobby.

> A mi madre le encanta viajar e ir de vacaciones. Le gusta prolongar la experiencia y por tanto dedica horas a organizar el viaje antes de ir. Primero, busca información en línea para ver qué tiempo hace en el país en el momento en que quiere ir, y lee información sobre todos los hoteles y apartamentos antes de reservar uno. Además, mira los mapas y las páginas de recomendaciones y, después, escribe una lista de todos los sitios que quiere visitar. Y eso no es todo. Cuando vuelve de las vacaciones, crea una presentación con todas sus fotos y comentarios porque le gusta tener un recuerdo de su viaje.

Answer the questions **in English**. You do not need to write in full sentences.

(a) Why does Sara's mother spend so long on holiday planning?

.... (1 mark)

(b) What does she do first?

.... (1 mark)

(c) What does she do after looking at maps and recommendations?

.... (1 mark)

(d) What does she make when she comes back?

.... (1 mark)

(e) Why does she like to do this?

.... (1 mark)

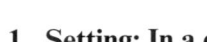

Media and technology

Had a go ☐   Nearly there ☐   Nailed it! ☐

Computer games

Role play

1 Setting: **In a computer shop**

Scenario:
- You are in a computer shop, buying a videogame.
- Play the recording to hear the teacher's role.
- You will hear questions **in Spanish** and you must answer **in Spanish** in the pauses.
- You are expected to say a few words or a short phrase / sentence in response to each prompt. One-word answers will not be sufficient to gain full marks.

> **Task:**
> 1 Say what you want to buy.
> 2 Say who it is for.
> 3 Say what type of game you want.
> 4 Give your opinion of computer games.
> 5 Ask the employee a question about cost.

> Try to vary your language and avoid repeating yourself. Instead of saying *quiero* for 'I want' every time, two useful alternatives to learn are *me gustaría* and *quisiera*, both of which mean 'I would like'.

(10 marks)

Playing computer games

2 Read the text about girls and computer games.

> En el pasado muy pocas chicas jugaban a los videojuegos, pero esto está cambiando rápidamente. Según un informe de la industria, un 46% de los jugadores en el mundo son chicas. Las cifras muestran que las chicas que juegan juegos sociales en los que cooperan* con amigas tendrán amistades más fuertes después. Es interesante notar que cuando las chicas juegan un videojuego con mucha violencia sienten más estrés** que los chicos. Por lo tanto, aunque muchas chicas eligen jugar a los videojuegos de aventura, suelen preferir los que tienen menos violencia.

*cooperan – (they) cooperate
**estrés – stress

Complete the sentences below.

Put a cross [×] in the correct box for each question.

(a) The text says that …

☐	**A** the gaming industry is targeting girls.
☐	**B** more girls play computer games than before.
☐	**C** games for girls were poor in the past.

(b) These days …

☐	**A** almost half the world's players are female.
☐	**B** there are 46% more girl players than ten years ago.
☐	**C** more and more games designers are women.

(c) Girls who play social games …

☐	**A** learn to be more competitive.
☐	**B** acquire computer skills they can use in later life.
☐	**C** develop firmer friendships.

(d) Violent games …

☐	**A** create more stress in girls than in boys.
☐	**B** are just as popular with girls as with boys.
☐	**C** can cause violent behaviour in both girls and boys.

(4 marks)

Had a go ☐ Nearly there ☐ Nailed it! ☐

Media and technology

The good and bad of technology

Picture task

1 Describe this picture.

Your description **must** cover:
- people
- location
- activity.

When you have finished your description, play the recording to hear and respond to two questions relating to the picture.

You are expected to say a few words or a short phrase / sentence in response to each question. One-word answers will not be sufficient to gain full marks. **(12 marks)**

> If you are not sure of one of the bullet points, it's absolutely fine to make a guess. For example, here, the photo could have been taken in the man's home or in the office. You could start by saying *No estoy seguro/a dónde está el hombre …* ('I'm not sure where the man is …') and then go on to say that you think he is in his house or in his office.

A letter about technology

2 Write a letter to your friend about technology.

You **must** include the following points:
- what you use the internet for
- your opinion of technology with reasons
- a problem you had with technology last week
- how you will use the internet this weekend.

> Make sure you do not repeat information, as you cannot receive marks for it twice. Because you can plan your work in advance, you can think about what information to use for each bullet point, ensuring that you don't use the same material twice.

Write your answer **in Spanish**. You should aim to write between 80 and 90 words.

....
....
....
....
....
....
....
....
....
....
....
....

(18 marks)

Free time — Had a go ☐ Nearly there ☐ Nailed it! ☐

Hobbies

Dictation

1 You are going to hear someone talking about their hobby.

Sentences 1–3: write down the missing words in the gaps provided. In each gap, you will write one word **in Spanish**.

Example: *Leo <u>libros</u> de <u>ciencia</u> ficción.*

1 Me ………………………… mucho el ………………………… .

2 A ………………………… voy al ………………………… .

3 Ver la ………………………… es ………………………… .

Sentences 4–6: write down the full sentences that you hear in the spaces provided, **in Spanish**.

Example: *<u>Le encanta ir al teatro.</u>*

4 ………………………………………………………… .

5 ………………………………………………………… .

6 ………………………………………………………… .   **(10 marks)**

Read aloud

2 Elena, your friend, has written about her hobbies. Read out the text below.

> Me interesa mucho el teatro y en el colegio me gusta participar en las obras que representamos.
> Quisiera ser actriz en el futuro.
> También me encanta jugar a los videojuegos porque hay algunos que son muy emocionantes.
> Con mi familia, me gusta relajarme y ver comedias en la televisión.

Once you have read the text, play the recording to hear and respond to two questions related to what you have read.

You are expected to say a few words or a short phrase / sentence in response to each question. One-word answers will not be sufficient to gain full marks.   **(12 marks)**

> You can hear a recording of the text and sample answers to the questions in the Answers section.

Had a go ☐ Nearly there ☐ Nailed it! ☐

Free time

Music and dance

Dance

1 Read this article about traditional dance in Spain.

> Mucha gente piensa que el flamenco es el baile tradicional de España, pero en realidad, es más típico del sur de España. Las varias regiones de España tienen sus propios bailes y están orgullosas de sus costumbres de música y baile. Por ejemplo, en la comunidad de Cataluña* el baile tradicional es la **Sardana**. Este baile se puede ver en las fiestas locales de los pueblos catalanes**, o durante los meses de verano, en la Plaza Sant Jaume 1*** en Barcelona los domingos por la tarde. Otro baile tradicional del norte de España es la **Jota****** que se baila acompañada del ritmo de las **castañuelas**. Se dice que este baile tiene sus orígenes en el siglo diecisiete.

*Cataluña – Catalonia, a region in northeast Spain
***Plaza Sant Jaume 1 – a square in Barcelona
**catalanes – Catalan (from / in Catalonia)
****Jota – a dance from the north of Spain

> If a text on a Reading paper refers to places or names that you may not know, then they will be 'glossed'. This means that there will be an asterisk that leads you to a translation or explanation of the name.

Complete the sentences below. Put a cross [×] in the correct box for each question.

(a) Flamenco …

☐ **A** is the Spanish national dance.
☐ **B** is a dance from the south of Spain.
☐ **C** is still danced by many people.

(b) The regions of Spain …

☐ **A** share the same customs.
☐ **B** all have hot weather.
☐ **C** are proud of their traditions.

(c) The *Sardana* is …

☐ **A** a regional dance.
☐ **B** traditional music.
☐ **C** a local festival.

(d) You can see the *Sardana* …

☐ **A** on some summer evenings.
☐ **B** most afternoons.
☐ **C** on Sunday mornings.

(e) Look at the second-to-last sentence again. What do you think **castañuelas** are?

☐ **A** costumes
☐ **B** musical instruments
☐ **C** dancers

(f) The dance called the *Jota* has its origins in …

☐ **A** the 16th century.
☐ **B** the 17th century.
☐ **C** the 18th century.

(6 marks)

A music article

2 Write an article about music.

You **must** include the following points:

- your favourite music
- when you listen to music
- a group / singer you would like to see.

Write your answer **in Spanish**. You should aim to write between 40 and 50 words.

> If you write 15 words for each bullet point, you have achieved the required word count. So you do not have to write a huge amount but you will need to extend each answer a little. You could give a reason (*porque* …) or give two responses (… *y también* …).

....

....

....

....

(14 marks)

Free time

Had a go ☐ Nearly there ☐ Nailed it! ☐

Music and dance events

A TV dance show

1 Marcos and Andrea are talking about a TV dance show.

What do they say?

Listen to the recording and complete the sentences by putting a cross [×] in the correct box for each question.

(a) Andrea thought that …

☐	**A** the public got the vote right.
☐	**B** the couple did not deserve to be last.
☐	**C** the standard throughout was excellent.

(1 mark)

(b) Marcos …

☐	**A** agrees with Andrea.
☐	**B** thinks the opposite of Andrea.
☐	**C** is not sure what to think.

(1 mark)

(c) Marcos was not impressed by …

☐	**A** the woman with the short hair.
☐	**B** the model with the curly hair.
☐	**C** the actor with the blonde hair.

(1 mark)

(d) He believes the public vote for …

☐	**A** someone who is funny.
☐	**B** a pleasant personality.
☐	**C** the best dancer.

(1 mark)

Translation

2 Translate the following sentences **into English**.

(a) Tengo las entradas para el concierto.

....

(b) Creo que va a ser muy emocionante.

....

(c) Mi grupo favorito tocará sus últimas canciones.

....

(d) Ayer escuché su música y leí la letra.

....

(e) Vamos a pasarlo muy bien, estoy segura.

.... **(10 marks)**

Had a go ☐ **Nearly there** ☐ **Nailed it!** ☐   **Free time**

Reading

Picture description

See this photo in colour

1 Describe this picture.

Your description **must** cover:
- people
- location
- activity.

When you have finished your description, play the recording to hear and respond to two questions relating to the picture.

You are expected to say a few words or a short phrase / sentence in response to each question. One-word answers will not be sufficient to gain full marks.   **(12 marks)**

> In the exam, if you forget to include one of the aspects that you need to describe, don't worry, your teacher is allowed to give you a prompt to remind you. They can say one of the following:
> - ¿(Y) la gente / la(s) persona(s)? And the people / the person?
> - ¿(Y) dónde está(n)? (And) where is he / she? / where are they?
> - ¿(Y) qué está(n) haciendo? (And) what are they doing? / what is he / she doing?

Translation

2 Translate the following sentences **into Spanish**.

(a) I don't like to read comedies.

....

(b) This book has too many pages.

....

(c) The main character is very nice.

....

(d) My brother prefers science fiction novels.

....

(e) Last week I read a book with a very sad ending.

....   **(10 marks)**

Free time

Had a go ☐   Nearly there ☐   Nailed it! ☐

Television

A letter about television

1 Write a letter to your friend about television.

You **must** include the following points:
- what sort of programmes you watch
- your opinion of one of your favourite programmes with reasons
- what you watched last week
- what you will watch this weekend.

> Notice that the regular format of this type of question requires an opinion with reasons, a past tense and a future tense. If you know what to expect in the exam, you know how to focus your learning and your revision.

Write your answer **in Spanish**. You should aim to write between 80 and 90 words.

………
………
………
………
………
………
………
………
………
………
………
………

(18 marks)

TV programmes tonight

2 A TV presenter is announcing this evening's programmes.

What does he say?

Listen to the recording and complete the sentences by putting a cross [×] in the correct box for each question.

Listen to the recording

(a) Later on you can see …

☐	**A** a dance show.
☐	**B** a drama series.
☐	**C** a song contest.

(b) The next programme is for people interested in …

☐	**A** history.
☐	**B** nature.
☐	**C** sport.

(2 marks)

Had a go ☐   Nearly there ☐   Nailed it! ☐   **Free time**

The cinema

Read aloud

1 Javier, your Spanish friend, has written to you about a film he has seen.

Read out the text below.

> Me gusta ir al cine, aunque cuesta mucho si compras bebidas y chocolate además de las entradas. Fui a ver una película el jueves pasado. Al principio pensé que era una comedia, pero tenía un final tan triste que era difícil no llorar. En general, prefiero las películas de terror.

Once you have read the text, play the recording and answer two questions related to what you have read.

You are expected to say a few words or a short phrase / sentence in response to each question. One-word answers will not be sufficient to gain full marks. **(12 marks)**

> The letters *j* and *g* (when *g* is followed by *e* or *i*) are pronounced like the 'ch' in the Scottish word 'loch'. Listen to the recording of the words *justo*, *tarjeta*, *colegio*, *página*, *coger*, *gente* and practise saying them.
>
> Other sounds tested in the passage include the words below. Listen to the rest of the recording and practise saying the words.
>
> (*cu* + vowel) *cuenta, cuidar, cuatro*   (*ci*) *cita, fácil, decir*   (*ll*) *llegar, calle, ella*

Track 28

Translation

2 Translate the paragraph **into Spanish**.

> My favourite film is the story of a woman who wants to be a star. It is a musical, with some wonderful songs, and it won a lot of prizes. Sometimes it is funny but it has some sad moments too. I am going to watch it again this weekend.

....
....
....
....
....
....
....
.... **(10 marks)**

> The translation on the Higher paper will contain an expression of past and future times as well as the present. There are 6 marks available for making the meaning clear and 4 marks for the accuracy of the vocabulary and grammar.

Free time

Had a go ☐ Nearly there ☐ Nailed it! ☐

What's the story?

TV and film

1 Nadim is talking about TV and film.

   What does he say?

   Complete the gap in each sentence using a word from the box below.

   There are more words than gaps.

   | comedy | adventure | action | horror |
   | friend | cousin | girlfriend |

   (a) On TV, Nadim likes to watch .... films. **(1 mark)**

   (b) In the cinema, he prefers .... films. **(1 mark)**

   (c) He goes to the cinema with his .... **(1 mark)**

Picture task

See this photo in colour

2 Describe the picture.

   Your description **must** cover:
   - people
   - location
   - activity.

   When you have finished your description, play the recording and answer the two questions relating to the picture.

   You are expected to say a few words or a short phrase / sentence in response to each question. One-word answers will not be sufficient to gain full marks. **(12 marks)**

Had a go ☐ Nearly there ☐ Nailed it! ☐   **Free time**

Celebrities and role models

Celebrities

1 Read this article from an online magazine.

> **Hugo González** es un cantante cubano que es muy popular en las redes sociales, no solo por su música. Sus aficionados lo respetan por lo que hace para ayudar a la gente que vive en la calle.
>
> **Alba Castro**, la actriz peruana, salió en una revista la semana pasada porque ha empezado una campaña para apoyar a las víctimas de la violencia. La actriz es un buen modelo de conducta.
>
> **Emilio Morales**, el jugador de fútbol boliviano, dedica unas horas cada semana para trabajar en un banco de comida cerca de su casa. Insiste que es lo menos que puede hacer.

Which question matches which person? Put a cross [×] in the correct column for each question.

	Who …	Hugo	Alba	Emilio	
(a)	… is Peruvian?				(1 mark)
(b)	… helps in a food bank?				(1 mark)
(c)	… is Cuban?				(1 mark)
(d)	… helps victims of violence?				(1 mark)
(e)	… is Bolivian?				(1 mark)
(f)	… helps the homeless?				(1 mark)

> It is a good idea to read through the question first so that you know what information you are looking for when you read the text. Then read the text all the way through before you start putting your crosses in the grid. As you read, you could underline the essential sections in the text where you have found key information for the answers.

A letter about a celebrity

2 Write a letter to your friend about your favourite celebrity.

You **must** include the following points:

- what the person looks like
- your opinion of whether the person is a good role model with reasons
- where you learned about or followed the person online recently
- where you will see the person in the future.

> This is a typical writing task of 80–90 words. You can expect to:
> - give a description
> - give an opinion
> - talk about something that happened in the past
> - mention something that will happen in the future.

Write your answer **in Spanish**. You should aim to write between 80 and 90 words.

....

....

....

....

....

....

....

(18 marks)

Local environment and transport

Had a go ☐ Nearly there ☐ Nailed it! ☐

Places in town

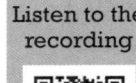

A podcast

1 Iván is talking in a podcast.

What does he say about his town?

Complete the gap in each sentence using a word or phrase from the box below. There are more words / phrases than gaps.

station	port	park	market
in the square	on the corner	on the outskirts	

(a) Iván lives near the .... (1 mark)

(b) He sometimes walks round the .... (1 mark)

(c) He often goes to the café .... (1 mark)

Role play

2 **Setting: In the street**

Scenario:

- You are in a Spanish town and you stop a passer-by. You are looking for the shops.
- Play the recording to hear the teacher's role.
- You will hear questions **in Spanish** and you must answer **in Spanish** in the pauses.
- You are expected to say a few words or a short phrase / sentence in response to each prompt. One-word answers will not be sufficient to gain full marks.

Task:
1 Say what sort of shop you are looking for.
2 Ask about shop opening times.
3 Ask for directions.
4 Say that you are also looking for somewhere to eat.
5 Say what sort of food you prefer.

(10 marks)

You can hear a sample complete role play in the Answers section.

> If you see a word that you can't remember, think how else you could get the same message across. For example, if you can't recall the verb 'to look for' (*buscar*) you could say 'I'd like to go to a supermarket' for the first task. For the fourth task, you could say 'I want to eat in a good restaurant'.

32

Had a go ☐ Nearly there ☐ Nailed it! ☐

Local environment and transport

Things to do in town

Plans for a visit

1 Alejandro is telling his cousin, Javier, what they will do when Javier comes to stay.

What does he say?

Listen to the recording and complete the sentences by putting a cross [×] in the correct box for each question.

(a) On the first day of Javier's visit they will …

☐	**A** go to the shopping centre.
☐	**B** go to the sports centre.
☐	**C** go to the café.

(b) On Friday they will …

☐	**A** go to the cinema.
☐	**B** go to the swimming pool.
☐	**C** go to the theatre.

(c) On Saturday they will …

☐	**A** eat out at a restaurant.
☐	**B** shop for birthday presents.
☐	**C** have a meal at home.

(d) On Sunday they will …

☐	**A** do some sport.
☐	**B** go for a walk.
☐	**C** visit the castle.

(4 marks)

> With this type of question, the wording at the start of each sentence gives you a key word to listen out for so that you know that the answer you need is about to be given. Listen out for the word 'first' (*primer* / *primero*) and the relevant days of the week.

Translation: This weekend

2 Translate the following sentences **into Spanish**.

(a) She will go shopping on Tuesday.

....

(b) He will visit the castle this weekend.

....

(c) I will eat in the café.

....

(d) Will you be able to play football on Saturday?

....

(e) I will watch a film in the square.

....

> Remember that to say 'on' a day of the week, just use *el* for a singular day and *los* for plural days. 'This' is either *este* (for a masculine singular noun) or *esta* (for a feminine singular noun).

(10 marks)

Local environment and transport

Had a go ☐ Nearly there ☐ Nailed it! ☐

Shopping for clothes

Shopping

1 Read what these people say about shopping.

Who says what? Choose the correct answers. Put a cross [×] in the correct column for each question.

Sara
No entiendo por qué a la gente le gusta ir de compras. El supermercado está bastante lejos de mi casa y siempre está lleno de gente. Por eso nunca voy allí, y hago la compra en la tienda que está al lado de mi casa porque es más práctico.

Luisa
Yo no soy aficionada a comprar. Sin embargo, me gusta estar a la moda. Muchos de mis amigos hacen fiestas para vender ropa y maquillaje*, y eso me gusta. ¡Ganan dinero también!

Javier
Normalmente compro en las tiendas de uno de los centros comerciales que hay en Burgos. Me encanta la variedad y suelen ser más baratos. ¡Es la mejor manera de comprar! De vez en cuando también compro por Internet.

maquillaje – make-up

	Who …	Sara	Luisa	Javier
(a)	… likes being in fashion?			
(b)	… never goes to the supermarket?			
(c)	… occasionally shops online?			
(d)	… prefers the local shops?			
(e)	… enjoys sales parties?			
(f)	… tends to go to shopping centres?			

(6 marks)

> Try to revise some vocabulary every day – it is much easier to learn five words a day than hundreds of words just before your exams! Try to use the *Revise* vocabulary tests every day – it will only take you a few minutes!

Role play

2 **Setting: In a clothes shop**

Scenario:
- You are in a clothes shop, talking to the shop assistant.
- Play the recording to hear the teacher's role.
- You will hear questions **in Spanish** and you must answer **in Spanish** in the pauses.
- You are expected to say a few words or a short phrase / sentence in response to each prompt. One-word answers will not be sufficient to gain full marks.

Listen to the recording

Task:
1 Say what you want to buy.
2 Say what size you want.
3 Say which colour you want.
4 Say what event you want the item of clothing for.
5 Ask a question about cost.

> Some vital words that can get you a long way in role plays are *quiero* (I want) and *¿cuánto?* (how much?)

(10 marks)

You can hear a sample of the full role play in the Answers section.

Had a go ☐ Nearly there ☐ Nailed it! ☐   **Local environment and transport**

Transport

Getting around

1 Translate the following paragraph **into English**.

> Para ir al colegio antes iba a pie, pero ahora voy en bicicleta porque es más rápido. Si quiero ir a la ciudad, suelo coger el autobús. No es tan cómodo como el tren y lleva cuarenta minutos, pero es mucho más barato. En la ciudad se puede tomar un barco para cruzar a la isla.

....
....
....
....
....
....
....

(10 marks)

> Remember that *suelo* comes from the verb *soler* and means 'to usually do something'. So if you say *Suelo ir al instituto a pie* you could translate it as 'I usually walk to school' or 'I usually go to school on foot'.

Picture task

See this photo in colour

2 Describe this picture.

Your description **must** cover:
- people
- location
- activity.

> Don't be afraid to use your imagination. What is the woman working on? Where are they going? Who is the man talking to? How do the other people feel about him talking on the phone?

When you have finished your description, play the recording and answer the two questions relating to the picture.

You are expected to say a few words or a short phrase / sentence in response to each question. One-word answers will not be sufficient to gain full marks.

(12 marks)

Listen to the recording

Local environment and transport

Had a go ☐   Nearly there ☐   Nailed it! ☐

Travel on public transport and buying tickets

Picture task

See this photo in colour

1   Describe the photo. Write four short sentences **in Spanish**.

.... (2 marks)
.... (2 marks)
.... (2 marks)
.... (2 marks)

> The photo for this task is always in colour so make sure you learn colours in Spanish. This will ensure you have a couple of things to describe straight away.

Role play

Listen to the recording

2   **Setting: At the bus station**

Scenario:
- You are at the bus station, talking to the employee.
- Play the recording to hear the teacher's role.
- You will hear questions **in Spanish** and you must answer **in Spanish** in the pauses.
- You are expected to say a few words or a short phrase / sentence in response to each prompt. One-word answers will not be sufficient to gain full marks.

Task:
1 Say where you want to go.
2 Say what time you prefer to go.
3 Say what type of tickets you want and how many.
4 Say why you are making the journey.
5 Ask a question about where the bus leaves from.

(10 marks)

You can hear a sample of the full role play in the Answers section.

> On the Foundation paper, the role play will only require present tenses or the common phrase *me gustaría* ('I would like'). There will be five bullet point tasks that you need to communicate and **one** question that you need to ask.

Had a go ☐ **Nearly there** ☐ **Nailed it!** ☐

Local environment and transport

My region – good and bad

Listen to the recording

Dictation

1 You are going to hear someone talking about their region.

Sentences 1–2: write down the missing words in the gaps provided. In each gap, you will write one word **in Spanish**.

Example: *En mi región hay muchos parques.*

1 Hay unos .... en la ....

2 El .... en las .... es muy ....

Sentences 3–6: write down the full sentences that you hear in the spaces provided, **in Spanish**.

Example: *Me encanta vivir en este barrio.*

3 ....
4 ....
5 ....
6 ....   **(10 marks)**

> In the Dictation you have to use your knowledge of the language and the grammar as well as simply recognising individual words. When you hear what sounds like 'athay' you need to remember the letter 'c' sounds like 'th' when it is followed by 'e'. (In fact, the letter combination 'th' doesn't exist in Spanish!) Then you need to recall the verb *hacer*, with the silent 'h' at the start. Put this knowledge together and you will realise that 'athay' is in fact *hace*.

A blog

2 Write a blog about the area where you live.

You **must** include the following points:

- how long you have lived there
- the pros and cons of the area
- what you did in the area last week
- what you and your friends will do in the area next weekend.

> Remember that you don't need to answer all the bullet points equally, as long as you do complete each task. It won't take you long to answer bullet point one, but there will be plenty for you to say in bullet points two to four.

Write your answer **in Spanish**. You should aim to write between 130 and 150 words.

....
....
....
....
....
....
....
....
....
....   **(22 marks)**

Local environment and transport

Had a go ☐ Nearly there ☐ Nailed it! ☐

My region in the past

Read aloud

1 Your friend, Sofía, has contributed to a blog about the history of her town.

Read out the text below.

> Mi abuela se acuerda de la ciudad en los años cincuenta.
> Dice que no había mucho tráfico porque casi nadie tenía coche.
> Iban a pie a todas partes.
> La gente trabajaba la tierra y era bastante pobre.
> El sentido de comunidad era muy fuerte y era una niña feliz.

Once you have read the text, play the recording and answer two questions related to what you have read.

You are expected to say a few words or a short phrase / sentence in response to each question. One-word answers will not be sufficient to gain full marks.

You can hear a sample recording of the text, questions and answers in the Answers section.

(12 marks)

> Remember to take care over double vowels. The Spanish combination of *ie* is very different to the English.
>
> In Spanish you can hear both sounds distinctly: *pie* is pronounced 'pee – eh'.
> In English 'ie' in 'pie' just sounds like 'eye'.

Translation

2 Translate the following sentences **into Spanish**.

(a) There are lots of fields in my region.

....

(b) We do not have green spaces in the city.

....

(c) The neighbours in my street are very friendly.

....

(d) I like the park next to the river.

....

(e) I used to live in a small village.

....

(10 marks)

> If a verb in the past is one word, you are likely to need the preterite tense ('we went', 'I saw', 'they found'). If the English sentence includes the words 'used to', as in (e) above, or 'was / were …ing', you will need the imperfect.

Had a go ☐ **Nearly there** ☐ **Nailed it!** ☐

Local environment and transport

Town or country?

My town

1 Héctor and Laura are talking about where they live. What do they say?

Put a cross [×] next to the **three** correct statements for each person.

(a) Héctor says that …

	A	his town, Gandía, is in the southeast of Spain.
☐	B	Gandía has sixty thousand inhabitants.
☐	C	the area was a lot greener in the past.
☐	D	they get a lot of tourists there.
☐	E	there are very few hotels.
☐	F	he wouldn't make any changes to his town.

> Be careful with numbers. It is easy to confuse *cinco* (five) with *cincuenta* (fifty), and *ocho* (eight) with *ochenta* (eighty). Also, make sure that you have heard the **whole** number. Laura says that there are **ciento** *cincuenta mil* inhabitants, not just *cincuenta mil*.

(b) Laura says that …

☐	A	Lanzarote has forty thousand inhabitants.
☐	B	the island is near Africa.
☐	C	there is a network of trains on the island.
☐	D	there are plenty of buses for the tourists.
☐	E	she wouldn't provide any more transport.
☐	F	the environment matters more.

(6 marks)

A tourist brochure

2 Read this extract from a tourist brochure.

> La costa del norte parece ser un secreto bien guardado porque, a pesar de su belleza, es una zona poco visitada por los turistas extranjeros. Sin embargo, muchos españoles han descubierto sus ventajas y vienen a la región para buscar la paz del campo y el placer de estar en contacto con la naturaleza. Aquí hay de todo, desde maravillosas playas de arena hasta montañas cubiertas de nieve. No muy lejos de la costa encontrarás numerosas ciudades históricas que vale la pena visitar.

Complete the sentences below.

Put a cross [×] in the correct box for each question.

(a) The north coast is described as …

☐	A	touristy.
☐	B	beautiful.
☐	C	rainy.

(b) The area …

☐	A	is popular with foreign tourists.
☐	B	gets few visitors.
☐	C	is appreciated by Spanish visitors.

(c) People go there to …

☐	A	go camping.
☐	B	get in touch with nature.
☐	C	escape the heat.

(d) The article mentions …

☐	A	small villages.
☐	B	sandy beaches.
☐	C	green fields.

(e) The cities are …

☐	A	not far from the coast.
☐	B	there on the coast.
☐	C	a long way inland.

> *Una zona poco visitada* means 'an area little visited' or 'an area not much visited'. The word *poco* ('little', 'few', 'not much') is key to understanding this phrase.

(5 marks)

Tourism

Had a go ☐   Nearly there ☐   Nailed it! ☐

Plans for the holidays

Holiday plans

1 Marta is talking about her holiday plans.

What does she say?

Complete the gap in each sentence using a word or phrase from the box below. There are more words / phrases than gaps.

> shopping   relaxing   working   getting up late
> on the coast   in the town centre   in a shop
> going on holiday   helping in the garden   going to bed late   walking

(a) Marta's first thought is of .... (1 mark)

(b) She then plans to spend the day .... (1 mark)

(c) Marta will continue her weekend job .... (1 mark)

(d) In August, she hopes to be .... (1 mark)

(e) In the good weather she will be .... (1 mark)

> Always listen out for key words that link to the questions – these will alert you to the fact that you are about to hear an answer. You could highlight key words in the exam in the preparation time at the start. Here, key words are: first, then, continue, August. The last question is trickier as the key words 'good weather' come after the answer.

A text conversation

2 Read Luis and Hugo's texts about holiday plans. Answer the questions **in English**. You don't need to write complete sentences.

> **Luis:** ¿Vamos a la piscina mañana?
> **Hugo:** Pero mañana es sábado, habrá demasiada gente. ¿El lunes?
> **Luis:** Los lunes está cerrada para limpiar. ¿Qué te parece si paseamos en bicicleta mañana y vamos a la piscina el martes?
> **Hugo:** Perfecto, y yo llevaré bocadillos y una bebida para nuestro almuerzo durante la excursión.

(a) Where does Luis first suggest they go?

.... (1 mark)

(b) Why does Hugo think it's a bad idea?

.... (1 mark)

(c) What day does Hugo suggest?

.... (1 mark)

(d) What is the problem with Hugo's suggestion?

.... (1 mark)

(e) What is Luis's new idea for tomorrow?

.... (1 mark)

(f) What will Hugo bring?

.... (1 mark)

Holiday preferences

Tourism

Had a go ☐ Nearly there ☐ Nailed it! ☐

My ideal holiday destination

1 Read these social media comments about the ideal holiday destination.

> **Lola:** Me gustaría ir al Reino Unido. Necesito practicar el inglés y es el sitio ideal para visitar edificios históricos.
>
> **David:** Para mí, el destino ideal sería África. Es un continente de paisajes muy diferentes y creo que la gente es muy simpática allí.
>
> **Alba:** Yo preferiría ir a las Islas Baleares. Hay mucho que hacer para los jóvenes y el viaje para llegar allí es muy corto.

Where would Lola, David and Alba like to go and why?

Complete the tables **in English**. You do not need to write in full sentences.

(a) Lola

Destination	....	(1 mark)
One reason	....	(1 mark)

(b) David

Destination	....	(1 mark)
One reason	....	(1 mark)

(c) Alba

Destination	....	(1 mark)
One reason	....	(1 mark)

> When an answer box asks you to give one reason, that means that there is more than one reason given in the passage. It is a good idea to look at both (or all the) reasons given so that you can choose the answer you are most confident about.

Conversation

2 After the Picture task in the exam, you won't see the general conversation questions written down, you will only hear your teacher asking them.

Here are some typical questions on the topic of holiday preferences. Think about how you would answer them. Then play the recording of the questions and pause the recording after each question to give your answer.

- ¿Adónde te gustaría ir más en el mundo? ¿Por qué?
- ¿Prefieres pasar las vacaciones en tu propio país o ir al extranjero?
- ¿Qué destino prefieres para las vacaciones – la costa o las montañas?
- ¿Qué piensas de pasar las vacaciones en una casa en el campo?
- ¿Prefieres ir de vacaciones con tus amigos o con la familia? ¿Por qué?
- ¿En qué estación del año prefieres ir de vacaciones?

Listen to the recording

Tourism

Had a go ☐ Nearly there ☐ Nailed it! ☐

Types of holidays

Holiday activities

1 Read the comments from an internet forum.

> **Fátima:** A mí me gusta más alquilar un coche para visitar las ciudades y los pueblos históricos. Me fascina visitar los edificios y monumentos construidos hace muchos años.
>
> **Luis:** Yo siempre busco vacaciones activas, pero en el campo. Por ejemplo, me gusta montar a caballo y hacer ciclismo.
>
> **Pilar:** En general prefiero pasar tiempo en la ciudad porque me gusta ver las tiendas, comprar ropa y recuerdos y comer en restaurantes buenos.

Who says what? Choose the correct answers.

Put a cross [×] in the correct column for each question.

	Who likes to …	Fátima	Luis	Pilar	
(a)	… go shopping?				(1 mark)
(b)	… be in the country?				(1 mark)
(c)	… rent a car?				(1 mark)
(d)	… eat out?				(1 mark)
(e)	… go sightseeing?				(1 mark)
(f)	… get some exercise?				(1 mark)

> With this type of comprehension task, the questions (a) to (f) do not come in the same order as the text. This means you need to look at the questions in turn, then scan the text to find a relevant word. Start with 'go shopping' from question (a), skim-read through the comments until you find a word that suggests shopping, then read the sentence in detail to make sure you have found the real answer.

Picture task

2 Describe this picture.

Your description **must** cover:
- people
- location
- activity.

See this photo in colour

tienda – tent
el bosque – wood / forest

Listen to the recording

When you have finished your description, play the recording to hear and respond to two questions relating to the picture.

You are expected to say a few words or a short phrase / sentence in response to each question. One-word answers will not be sufficient to gain full marks.

(12 marks)

Had a go ☐ **Nearly there** ☐ **Nailed it!** ☐   **Tourism**

Where to stay

Talking about where to stay on holiday

1 Elena, Javier and Indra are talking about where they prefer to stay on holiday.

What do they say?

Listen to the recording and complete the sentences by putting a cross [×] in the correct box for each question.

(a) Elena and her family prefer an apartment because …

☐	**A** it's more private.
☐	**B** it's cheaper than a hotel.
☐	**C** it gives them more room.

(b) Elena says that having an apartment means …

☐	**A** you can cook when you want.
☐	**B** you can eat in different places.
☐	**C** you have more freedom.

(c) Javier's family think that being in a five-star hotel means you get …

☐	**A** bigger rooms.
☐	**B** excellent service.
☐	**C** better food.

(d) In a five-star hotel, there is …

☐	**A** a wide range of facilities.
☐	**B** room service.
☐	**C** 24-hour reception.

(e) Indra's idea of a perfect holiday is …

☐	**A** on a campsite with facilities.
☐	**B** camping in the woods.
☐	**C** in a house in the country.

(f) Indra wants …

☐	**A** to be close to restaurants and a pool.
☐	**B** to have modern washing facilities.
☐	**C** to get back to nature.

(6 marks)

> This is a multiple-choice style question and you will see these a lot in the Listening exam. At Foundation tier, there are four questions in this style with approximately 14 marks in total. At Higher tier there are three questions with a total of 13 marks. All the options will be plausible, so you need to listen carefully to eliminate the wrong answers and select the correct one. If you really don't know the answer, guess! You have a 33% chance of getting it right, whereas a blank box is definitely wrong.

Translation

2 Translate the following sentences **into Spanish**.

> In sentence (d) you need the imperfect as the verbs are ongoing. In sentence (e) the events are over; you need the preterite.

(a) The facilities in the hotel are excellent.

....

(b) We are going to stay in a five-star campsite.

....

(c) I hope to rent a house close to the beach.

....

(d) The apartment was very clean, and it had a view of the pool.

....

(e) It rained on Thursday and we went to the games room.

....

(10 marks)

Tourism

Had a go ☐ Nearly there ☐ Nailed it! ☐

Booking accommodation

Role play

Target grade 1–5

Listen to the recording

1 **Setting: At the hotel**

   Scenario:
   - You are in a hotel, trying to book a room.
   - Play the recording to hear the teacher's role.
   - You will hear questions **in Spanish**, and you must answer **in Spanish** in the pauses.
   - You are expected to say a few words or a short phrase / sentence in response to each prompt. One-word answers will not be sufficient to gain full marks.

   Task:
   1 Say what type of room you want.
   2 Say for how many nights.
   3 Say what view you want to have.
   4 Say when you want to eat.
   5 Ask what time the restaurant opens.

   (10 marks)

   > Lots of role plays involve you asking for something, so learn useful vocabulary like *Quiero …* ('I want'), *Me gustaría …* ('I would like') and *Quisiera …* ('I would like').
   >
   > You also need to ask a question or two, so make sure you study question words and phrases. Here you will need *¿A qué hora …?*

Dictation

Target grade 1–5

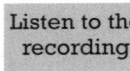

Listen to the recording

2 You are going to hear someone talking about holiday accommodation.

   Sentences 1–3: write down the missing words in the gaps provided. In each gap, you will write one word **in Spanish**.

   Example: *La sala de <u>juegos</u> es <u>pequeña</u>.*

   1 Las ………………………………………… son bastante ………………………………… .

   2 Quiero una ………………………………………… con ………………………………………… .

   3 Está ………………………………………… de la ………………………………………… .

   Sentences 4–6: write down the full sentences that you hear in the spaces provided, **in Spanish**.

   Example: *<u>Me gustaría reservar una mesa.</u>*

   4 ……………………………………………………………………………………………… .
   5 ……………………………………………………………………………………………… .
   6 ……………………………………………………………………………………………… .

   (10 marks)

   > Remember that when you hear a sound like the 'ni' in 'o**ni**on', this is the letter **ñ** in Spanish. You have come across it lots of times in words like *España* and *español*.

Had a go ☐ Nearly there ☐ Nailed it! ☐   **Tourism**

Holiday activities

Picture task

See this photo in colour

If at first glance you think there isn't enough to say, keep looking. You can mention: how many people there are, some of their clothes, where they are, what they are doing, the weather, the colour of the sky and if the people are happy or sad.

1   Describe the photo. Write four short sentences **in Spanish**.

    .... **(2 marks)**

    .... **(2 marks)**

    .... **(2 marks)**

    .... **(2 marks)**

2   **Read aloud**

Alba, your Argentinian friend, has written about her holiday.

Read out the text below.

> Ayer paseamos en bicicleta y hoy vamos a montar a caballo.
> Queremos alquilar un barco mañana después de jugar al tenis.
> Hace cuatro días fuimos a unos jardines hermosos.
> El perro estaba muy contento allí.

Listen to the recording

Once you have read the text, play the recording and answer two questions related to what you have read.

You are expected to say a few words or a short phrase / sentence in response to each question. One-word answers will not be sufficient to gain full marks. **(12 marks)**

> Remember that in the combinations of letters *que* and *qui* the 'u' sound is not pronounced, so you get *keh* and *ki* (not *kweh* and *kwi*).
>
> It is when *c* is followed by *u* that the 'u' sound **does** get pronounced (as in *cuatro, escuela* and *cuidar*).
>
> Listen to these words in the recording and repeat them for practice: Track 47
>
> *que, queremos, pequeño*
>
> *quitar, tranquilo, equipo*
>
> *cuatro, escuela, cuidar*

Tourism

Had a go ☐ Nearly there ☐ Nailed it! ☐

Trips and visits

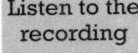

Role play

1 **Setting:** At the tourist office

Scenario:
- You are at the tourist office, talking to the employee.
- Play the recording to hear the teacher's role.
- You will hear questions **in Spanish** and you must answer **in Spanish** in the pauses.
- You are expected to say a few words or a short phrase / sentence in response to each prompt. One-word answers will not be sufficient to gain full marks.

> **Task:**
> 1 Say which day you would like to go on a trip.
> 2 Say what time you want to go.
> 3 Say what sort of trip you would like.
> 4 Ask about the price of the tickets.
> 5 Ask a question about when you will get back.

(10 marks)

> You can't know exactly what the teacher's role is going to be, so you cannot be sure exactly how the questions or comments by the teacher will be phrased. For this reason, you should prepare a full phrase or sentence for each point. So for the first point, don't just say *jueves* (Thursday). You need to say, in Spanish, 'I would like to go on a trip on Thursday' or 'I want to go on a trip on Thursday'.

Translation: A trip

2 Translate the following paragraph **into English**.

> Hace varios días, hicimos una excursión a las montañas al norte de la ciudad. Fuimos en autobús y el viaje duró una hora y media. Nos paramos en un pueblo para comer y había nieve por todas partes. Hoy estamos comprando recuerdos en el mercado, pero mañana tengo muchas ganas de visitar el castillo.

....
....
....
....
....
....
....
....
....
....

(10 marks)

> Avoid gaps if at all possible. For instance, if you don't know *nos paramos*, but you know everything else that is around the verb, then give a translation that makes sense instead of leaving a gap. Educated guesswork is a very useful skill!

Had a go ☐ Nearly there ☐ Nailed it! ☐   **Tourism**

Giving or asking for directions

Role play

1 **Setting: In town**

   Scenario:
   - You are in town, asking a passer-by for help.
   - Play the recording to hear the teacher's role.
   - You will hear questions **in Spanish** and you must answer **in Spanish** in the pauses.
   - You are expected to say a few words or a short phrase / sentence in response to each prompt. One-word answers will not be sufficient to gain full marks.

   > **Task:**
   > 1 Ask a question about the shop opening times.
   > 2 Say what your nationality is.
   > 3 Say what you think of the town.
   > 4 Say where you are staying.
   > 5 Say when you are returning home.

   (10 marks)

   > If you forget how to say 'to stay', you can get round it by saying, in Spanish, 'We are in the Hotel + name' (*Estamos en el Hotel…*) or 'We have a house / flat near the beach' (*Tenemos una casa / un piso cerca de la playa*).

Getting instructions

2 Read Mario's instructions on how to get to the café to meet him.

   > Sal de la casa y sigue la calle a la derecha. Al final, cruza el puente. Después, continúa hasta la biblioteca y toma la calle a la izquierda. A unos cincuenta metros, al lado del parque, está el Café Carmen. Te veré allí a las siete.

   Answer the questions **in English**. You do not need to write in full sentences.

   (a) What should you do on leaving the house?

   .... **(1 mark)**

   (b) What must you do at the end of the street?

   .... **(1 mark)**

   (c) What do you do when you reach the library?

   .... **(1 mark)**

   (d) How far along the street is the café?

   .... **(1 mark)**

   (e) What is next to the café?

   .... **(1 mark)**

   (f) What time will he be there?

   .... **(1 mark)**

Tourism

Had a go ☐   Nearly there ☐   Nailed it! ☐

Shopping for gifts

Picture task

1 Describe this picture.

Your description **must** cover:
- people
- location
- activity.

When you have finished your description, play the recording to hear and respond to two questions relating to the picture.

You are expected to say a few words or a short phrase / sentence in response to each question. One-word answers will not be sufficient to gain full marks.

(12 marks)

> Remember that the present continuous tense is really useful in the Picture task because you need to describe what people **are doing**.
>
> *Está mirando* – He / She is looking at
>
> *Están comprando* – They are buying
>
> *Están haciendo la compra* – They are doing the shopping

A conversation in a shop

2 Jalil is talking to a shop assistant.

What do they say?

Listen to the recording and complete the sentences by putting a cross [×] in the correct box for each question.

(a) Jalil wants to buy a book of ...

☐	**A**	short stories.
☐	**B**	local history.
☐	**C**	village customs.

(b) The shop assistant recommends the first book because of its ...

☐	**A**	colour photos.
☐	**B**	cheap price.
☐	**C**	famous author.

(c) The second book is recommended because ...

☐	**A**	there are more pages.
☐	**B**	the content is ideal.
☐	**C**	it is not as big.

(d) Jalil decides ...

☐	**A**	to get the first book.
☐	**B**	to buy both books.
☐	**C**	to take the second book.

(4 marks)

> Remember that *historia* can mean both 'story' and 'history'. In question 2(a) you will need to listen carefully to the other information in order to choose the correct answer.

Had a go ☐   Nearly there ☐   Nailed it! ☐   **Tourism**

Tourist information

Dictation

1 You are going to hear someone talking about tourist information.

Sentences 1–2: write down the missing words in the gaps provided. In each gap, you will write one word **in Spanish**.

Example: *El hotel está <u>cerca</u> del <u>centro</u> <u>comercial</u>.*

1 El .... es muy ....

2 No se permiten .... en el ....

Sentences 3–6: write down the full sentences that you hear in the spaces provided, **in Spanish**.

Example: <u>*Se puede visitar el barrio antiguo.*</u>

3 ....

4 ....

5 ....

6 ....   **(10 marks)**

> Use your understanding of the language to help you separate words. When we speak, we naturally run words into each other, especially when one word ends with a consonant and the next word begins with a vowel. So if you hear what sounds like 'vana', it is probably a vowel!

Translation

2 Translate the following sentences **into Spanish**.

(a) I am going to the tourist office.

....

> The mark scheme will always make it clear when there is more than one way to translate a word and you will be credited if you convey the correct meaning. For instance, both *enseñar* and *mostrar* mean 'to show'. (Remember that *mostrar* has a stem change: *o* to *ue*). For 'map', you could use either *el mapa* or *el plano*.

(b) We want a list of hotels in the area.

....

(c) The map shows many interesting places.

....

(d) Yesterday my brother and I hired bikes.

....

(e) The castle is not open to the public.

....   **(10 marks)**

49

Tourism

Had a go ☐ Nearly there ☐ Nailed it! ☐

Tourist attractions

Translation

1 Translate the following paragraph **into English**.

> Acabamos de pasar el día en Barcelona. Sin duda, es una ciudad hermosa con muchos sitios de interés. Disfruté paseando por la gran calle desde la plaza hasta el puerto, con los puestos de flores y los numerosos cafés. Vale la pena ir a ver el parque y los edificios. La arquitectura es muy interesante.

....
....
....
....
....
....

(10 marks)

> There will be some challenging parts of the translation at Higher tier, but there will also be some more straightforward parts. The translation, like all parts of the Higher paper, is designed to test ability ranges from grade 4 up to grade 9. So don't panic at the trickier bits, and attempt as much as you can.

A letter about tourist attractions

2 Write a letter to your Spanish friend about the local tourist attractions.

You **must** include the following points:
- what there is to see in the town
- your opinion of the countryside near you
- what you did in the city last week
- an activity that your friend can do when they visit.

> For the last bullet point you could suggest an activity you and your friend could do together:
>
> *Durante tu visita, ¿por qué no vamos a …?* (During your visit, why don't we go to …?)
>
> *Durante tu visita, hay un concierto / una fiesta. ¿Quieres ir?* (During your visit, there is a concert / a party. Do you want to go?)

Write your answer **in Spanish**. You should aim to write between 80 and 90 words.

....
....
....
....
....
....
....
....

(18 marks)

Had a go ☐   Nearly there ☐   Nailed it! ☐

Tourism

Holiday problems

A hotel review

1 Read this review by a customer of a hotel.

> No estaba contento con el hotel y no volvería. Varias veces, cuando comimos en el restaurante, la comida estaba fría. También, el primer día que llegamos, vimos que el baño de la habitación estaba sucio. Lo limpiaron después, pero no nos dio una buena imagen del hotel. La luz al lado de la cama no funcionaba y nunca la arreglaron mientras estuve allí.

Put a cross [×] in each one of the three correct boxes.

The customer says that …

☐	A	the bathroom was dirty.
☐	B	the bed was not comfortable.
☐	C	the bedside light did not work.
☐	D	the food was cold.
☐	E	the staff were not pleasant.
☐	F	the window was broken.

> Don't just rely on the information from one word. You might see the verb *limpiar* and recognise that it means 'to clean'. This could mislead you. When you read around you will find that they had to clean the room because it was dirty.

(3 marks)

A holiday blog

2 Write a blog about holidays.

You **must** include the following points:

- what sort of holiday you like
- the pros and cons of having a holiday in your own country
- a problem that you had on holiday in the past
- where you would like to visit in the future.

Write your answer **in Spanish**. You should aim to write between 130 and 150 words.

....

(22 marks)

Tourism

Had a go ☐ Nearly there ☐ Nailed it! ☐

Accommodation problems

Camping problems

1 Nicolás is speaking to the campsite receptionist.

Listen to the recording and answer the following questions **in English**. You do not need to write in full sentences.

(a) Who is Nicolás camping with?

.... **(1 mark)**

(b) Whereabouts on the site are they camping?

.... **(1 mark)**

(c) Why are they having trouble sleeping?

.... **(1 mark)**

(d) What rule are some young people breaking?

.... **(1 mark)**

(e) What is Nicolás's first idea for a solution?

.... **(1 mark)**

(f) What is his preferred solution?

.... **(1 mark)**

> Always read the questions carefully before the recording begins. It can help to highlight key words in the questions, and this ensures you do read them properly instead of skim-reading.

Translation

2 Translate the following sentences **into Spanish**.

(a) There is a problem with the bill.

....

(b) The knives in the apartment are dirty.

....

(c) Do you have a double room?

....

(d) We asked for a room with a view of the sea.

....

(e) I am not happy with the room.

.... **(10 marks)**

> Remember that *pedir* means 'to ask **for**', so you don't need an extra word to translate 'for'.
>
> Don't forget to make adjectives agree: for example, 'dirty' needs to agree with the noun it describes.

Had a go ☐ **Nearly there** ☐ **Nailed it!** ☐   **Tourism**

Eating out

Role play

1 **Setting: In the café**

   Scenario:
   - You are in a café in Spain, ordering food.
   - Play the recording to hear the teacher's role.
   - You will hear questions **in Spanish** and you must answer **in Spanish** in the pauses.
   - You are expected to say a few words or a short phrase / sentence in response to each prompt. One-word answers will not be sufficient to gain full marks.

   > **Task:**
   > 1 Say where you would like to sit.
   > 2 Say what you would like to eat.
   > 3 Say what you want to drink.
   > 4 Give your opinion of the food.
   > 5 Ask a question about the bill.

   (10 marks)

   You can hear a sample of the full role play in the Answers section.

   > Remember that it is perfectly all right to use vocabulary that is not on the Edexcel vocabulary list in the Speaking and Writing tasks. So if you know words for food and drink that are not on the list, you can certainly use them, as long as they are correct.

A restaurant conversation

2 Julia is talking to a waiter in the restaurant.

   Answer the following questions **in English**. You do not need to write in full sentences.

   (a) What does Julia first ask for?

   .... **(1 mark)**

   (b) Where is her table?

   .... **(1 mark)**

   (c) What does Julia want to know?

   .... **(1 mark)**

   (d) What does the waiter tell her?

   .... **(1 mark)**

   (e) What does her friend want to eat?

   .... **(1 mark)**

   (f) What do they order to drink?

   .... **(1 mark)**

Tourism

Had a go ☐ Nearly there ☐ Nailed it! ☐

Opinions about food

Picture task

1 Describe this picture.

Your description **must** cover:
- people
- location
- activity.

When you have finished your description, play the recording to hear and respond to two questions relating to the picture.

You are expected to say a few words or a short phrase / sentence in response to each question. One-word answers will not be sufficient to gain full marks.

(12 marks)

> During the preparation time, make sure you jot down ideas in Spanish about the three key things you must mention: the people, the location and the activity. If you forget to mention one of them, your teacher will remind you by asking:
>
> ¿Y la gente? (people)
>
> ¿Y dónde están? (location)
>
> ¿Y qué están haciendo? (activity)

Dictation

2 You are going to hear someone talking about eating out.

Sentences 1–3: write down the missing words in the gaps provided. In each gap, you will write one word **in Spanish**.

Example: *El café está frío*.

1 La .... está muy ....

2 Soy .... a los ....

3 Aquí .... churros ....

Sentences 4–6: write down the full sentences that you hear in the spaces provided, **in Spanish**.

Example: *Me gusta la comida vegana.*

4 ....

5 ....

6 .... **(10 marks)**

> When two vowels come together, you will hear each one.
> In *paella*, both the *a* and *e* sounds are heard. In *demasiado* you can hear the *i* and the *a*. In *prefiero* you will hear the *i* and the *e*.

Had a go ☐ Nearly there ☐ Nailed it! ☐

Tourism

The weather

Picture task

See this photo in colour

1 Describe the photo. Write four short sentences **in Spanish**.

.... **(2 marks)**

.... **(2 marks)**

.... **(2 marks)**

.... **(2 marks)**

> You may not know all the words for the clothes the people are wearing, but you can mention *el jersey* (jumper) and *la chaqueta* (jacket), or even *mucha ropa* (a lot of clothes)! You know that 'man' is *hombre*, and 'snow' is *nieve*, so a snowman will be a 'man of snow'.

Translation

2 Translate the sentences **into English**.

(a) Hace frío hoy y creo que va a nevar.

....

(b) Hay riesgo de temperaturas muy altas.

....

(c) Mañana hará calor y sol todo el día.

....

(d) Hizo mucho viento en la costa ayer.

....

(e) Está lloviendo y hay muchas nubes grises en el cielo.

....

> Be careful with the tenses in these sentences. There are verbs in the present (a, b and e), the future (c), the immediate future (a) and the preterite (d).

(10 marks)

Tourism

Had a go ☐ Nearly there ☐ Nailed it! ☐

Customs and festivals

St George's Day

1 Read this extract from a website about Barcelona.

> Según la tradición, el veintitrés de abril, o el Día de Sant Jordi, los hombres dan rosas a sus novias y las mujeres responden regalando un libro a su novio. Cada año, las calles y las plazas de Barcelona se llenan de puestos de libros. Los vendedores* llegan temprano para preparar los puestos y durante el día la gente visita los puestos para buscar el libro que quiere. A veces, hay un momento de emoción cuando el escritor o la escritora de un libro se presenta para firmar** copias de su libro para las personas que los compran.
>
> La fiesta primero se celebró el 7 de octubre de 1926, pero luego la cambiaron al 23 de abril por ser el día en que murieron*** dos de los escritores más famosos del mundo, el español Miguel de Cervantes (autor de *Don Quijote*****) y el escritor inglés William Shakespeare.

vendedores – seller
**firmar* – to sign
***murieron* – (they) died
****Don Quijote* – a novel written by the Spanish author Cervantes in the 17th century

Answer the following questions **in English**. You do not need to write in full sentences.

(a) What two gifts are traditionally given on 23 April?

.... **(2 marks)**

(b) What happens to the streets and squares of Barcelona on that day?

.... **(1 mark)**

(c) What happens early on the day?

.... **(1 mark)**

(d) What exciting event sometimes happens?

.... **(1 mark)**

(e) What is significant about 7 October 1926?

.... **(1 mark)**

(f) Why was the event moved?

.... **(1 mark)**

The April Fair

2 Sofía is talking about her visit to the April Fair in Seville, a city in the south of Spain.

What aspects does she mention?

Listen to the recording and put a cross [×] in each one of the **three** correct boxes.

☐	**A**	costumes
☐	**B**	dancing
☐	**C**	food
☐	**D**	horse parade
☐	**E**	singing
☐	**F**	weather

(3 marks)

Had a go ☐ **Nearly there** ☐ **Nailed it!** ☐   **Tourism**

A visit to Barcelona

Places of interest in Barcelona

1 Sara, Miguel and Ana are discussing what to see during their visit to Barcelona.

What do they say?

Listen to the recording and complete the sentences by putting a cross [×] in the correct box for each question.

(a) Sara wants to …

☐	**A** go to the sports centre.
☐	**B** visit the football stadium.
☐	**C** watch a football match.

(1 mark)

(b) Miguel wants to …

☐	**A** see the old part of town.
☐	**B** go the new shopping centre.
☐	**C** stroll down to the port.

(1 mark)

(c) Ana wants to take photos for her …

☐	**A** social media page.
☐	**B** art class.
☐	**C** history project.

> When more than one person speaks on a recording, you will always hear their names announced so that it is absolutely clear who is speaking.

(1 mark)

A recommendation for Barcelona

2 Read Sofía's suggestion for a place to visit in Barcelona.

> Cuando nos visitan amigos en Barcelona, siempre los llevamos al *Poble Espanyol* (o Pueblo Español) cerca de la Plaza de España en la ciudad. Es una especie de museo al aire libre con edificios que son copias de monumentos famosos de otras ciudades españolas. También hay edificios que representan los estilos de arquitectura que son típicos de otras provincias del país. Hay más de cien edificios en total, construidos en una red de calles y plazas ideales para pasear. Si quieres saber más, hay un sitio web con más información.

Complete the sentence below.

Put a cross [×] in each one of the **three** correct boxes.

The 'Pueblo Español' …

☐	**A** is a museum in a village near Barcelona.
☐	**B** has copies of famous Spanish monuments.
☐	**C** has examples of building styles from other parts of Spain.
☐	**D** has more than 150 buildings to see.
☐	**E** is a great place to stroll around.
☐	**F** is still constructing its visitor website.

> When selecting the options, make sure that the whole sentence or phrase is correct. For instance, the 'Pueblo Español' can be described as a sort of museum, but option A says it's in a village near Barcelona. Is that correct?

(3 marks)

Tourism

Had a go ☐ Nearly there ☐ Nailed it! ☐

A visit to Buenos Aires

A tourist website

1 Read this entry from a tourist website.

> Uno de los aspectos de la cultura argentina que ha ganado popularidad mundial es un baile que se llama tango. Este baile se desarrolló en la zona del río que forma una frontera entre los países de Argentina y Uruguay*. Al principio, era un baile popular entre las clases bajas de la ciudad de Buenos Aires, especialmente donde había un alto nivel de inmigración. Ahora se puede ver en espectáculos, clases y competiciones internacionales.

*Uruguay – a country in South America

Complete the sentences.

Put a cross [×] in the correct box for each question.

(a) The focus of the text is …

	A a dance.
	B a country's history.
	C poverty in Argentina.

(b) The border between Argentina and Uruguay is …

	A mountainous.
	B a river.
	C very long.

(c) The tango began …

	A as a country dance.
	B among the lower classes.
	C in the 18th century.

(d) Originally, it was especially popular …

	A for ballroom competitions.
	B in dance shows.
	C in areas of high immigration.

(4 marks)

Picture task

2 Describe this picture.

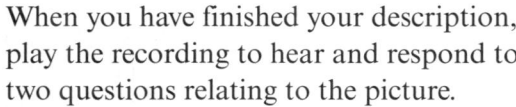

Your description **must** cover:
- people
- location
- activity.

When you have finished your description, play the recording to hear and respond to two questions relating to the picture.

You are expected to say a few words or a short phrase / sentence in response to each question. One-word answers will not be sufficient to gain full marks.

(12 marks)

> If you are asked about a city you have visited, it does not have to be a place abroad. It can be a town you have stayed in, somewhere you went to on a day trip or your own town. You can always find something to say about what you did there. Also, remember to stick to the vocabulary that you know – if you went paintballing the last time you went into town, it would be better to talk about other activities if you don't know a lot of the vocabulary you would need for that.

Had a go ☐ Nearly there ☐ Nailed it! ☐

My school

School subjects

In class

1 These teachers are talking in class. Which subject are they teaching?

Listen to the recording and put a cross [×] in the correct box for each question.

(a) ☐ **A** Art
    ☐ **B** Geography
    ☐ **C** History

> The subject is not mentioned by name but there are clues in what each teacher says that will lead you to the correct answer.

(1 mark)

(b) ☐ **A** Science
    ☐ **B** Religion
    ☐ **C** P.E.

(1 mark)

(c) ☐ **A** Maths
    ☐ **B** English
    ☐ **C** Music

(1 mark)

Read aloud

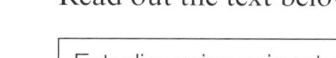

2 Emilio, your Peruvian friend, tells you about the subjects he studies.

Read out the text below.

> Estudio varias asignaturas y, al final del curso, tengo que escoger las que quiero hacer el año próximo.
> Me gustan las lenguas, y pienso continuar con el inglés.
> Saco buenas notas en matemáticas, pero la clase de educación física es mi favorita.
> Voy a dejar la historia porque nunca consigo aprenderme las fechas.

Once you have read the text, play the recording and answer two questions related to what you have read.

You are expected to say a few words or a short phrase / sentence in response to each question. One-word answers will not be sufficient to gain full marks. **(12 marks)**

You can hear a sample recording of the text, questions and answers in the Answers section.

> Remember to pronounce the letter 'v' as if it were a 'b' (in *voy* and *varias*).
> When Spanish children learn to write they often make the mistake of spelling these words with an initial 'b' because of the pronunciation.
> Listen to and repeat these words: *voy, varias, viernes, visto*.
> The letter *h* is silent unless it follows *c* (pronounced like 'ch' in 'church').
> Listen to and repeat these words: *hermano, historia, hotel, dicho, fecha, escuchar*.

Track 63

59

My school

Had a go ☐   Nearly there ☐   Nailed it! ☐

School subjects – likes and dislikes

Listen to the recording

Dictation

1 You are going to hear someone talking about their studies.

Sentences 1–2: write down the missing words in the gaps provided. In each gap, you will write one word **in Spanish**.

Example: *Se me <u>dan</u> muy <u>bien</u> las <u>matemáticas</u>.*

1 Normalmente .... buenas .... en ....

2 No tengo .... en .... pero es ....

Sentences 3–6: write down the full sentences that you hear in the spaces provided, **in Spanish**.

Example: *Me encanta la clase de dibujo.*

3 ....

4 ....

5 ....

6 .... **(10 marks)**

> Always look at the introduction to the task so that you know the topic that the sentences are about. This gives the sentences a context and you will begin to anticipate the range of vocabulary that you might hear.

A letter about school subjects

2 Write a letter to your friend about your school subjects.

You **must** include the following points:

- what subjects you study
- your opinion of one of your subjects with reasons
- what subject you dropped in the past
- what you will study next year.

> To achieve the top band of marks, you need to address all the bullet points, develop your ideas and show some variety of vocabulary and phrases.

Write your answer **in Spanish**. You should aim to write between 80 and 90 words.

....

....

....

....

....

....

....

....

.... **(18 marks)**

Had a go ☐   Nearly there ☐   Nailed it! ☐   **My school**

The school day

My school

1 Read these comments from an internet forum.

> **Andrea:** Mi colegio está bastante lejos y tengo que ir en autobús. Es un problema porque no puedo participar en las actividades después de las clases porque tengo que coger el autobús.
>
> **Iván:** En mi instituto, tenemos una hora para comer y las clases solo terminan a las cuatro menos diez. Preferiría continuar sin pausa y terminar antes.
>
> **Dani:** Durante el descanso, nos gusta salir al patio al aire libre. Allí hablamos con los amigos y comemos un bocadillo. Pero no hay ningún sitio para sentarnos. El instituto necesita poner unas mesas y sillas en el patio.

Who says what? Choose the correct answers.

Put a cross [×] in the correct column for each question.

	Who …	Andrea	Iván	Dani	
(a)	… has a long lunch hour?				(1 mark)
(b)	… can't walk to school?				(1 mark)
(c)	… has a snack at break?				(1 mark)
(d)	… wants better facilities outside?				(1 mark)
(e)	… can't join in the school clubs?				(1 mark)
(f)	… wants to shorten the school day?				(1 mark)

My school day

2 Write a letter to your friend about the school day.

You **must** include the following points:
- when classes start and finish
- your opinion of the after-school clubs or activities
- how you went to school yesterday
- what lessons you have tomorrow.

> It doesn't matter if you write a lot about one bullet point and less on another. As long as you answer all points, the balance doesn't matter.

Write your answer **in Spanish**. You should aim to write between 80 and 90 words.

....

....

....

....

....

....

....

....

....

....

.... **(18 marks)**

My school

Had a go ☐   Nearly there ☐   Nailed it! ☐

School facilities

One school's facilities

1 Read these comments from students about the advantages and disadvantages of the school's facilities.

> **Karima:** Lo bueno del colegio es que el gimnasio es muy moderno. Lo malo es que no tenemos suficientes ordenadores.
>
> **Daniel:** Me parece que tenemos una biblioteca excelente y que es un sitio ideal para estudiar. El aspecto que no me gusta es el patio porque es demasiado pequeño.
>
> **Leya:** Gracias al colegio por organizar un intercambio en el extranjero – es una oportunidad increíble. Un problema en mi opinión es que no hay clubs después de las clases.

What do they tell us? Complete the tables **in English**. You do not need to write in full sentences.

(a) Karima

Advantage	....
Disadvantage	....

(2 marks)

(b) Daniel

Advantage	....
Disadvantage	....

(2 marks)

(c) Leya

Advantage	....
Disadvantage	....

(2 marks)

Picture task

2 Describe the photo.

Write four short sentences **in Spanish**.

See this photo in colour

.... (2 marks)
.... (2 marks)
.... (2 marks)
.... (2 marks)

Had a go ☐ Nearly there ☐ Nailed it! ☐   **My school**

School uniform

Picture task

1 Describe this picture.

   Your description **must** cover:
   - people
   - location
   - activity.

See this photo in colour

When you have finished your description, play the recording to hear and respond to two questions relating to the picture.

You are expected to say a few words or a short phrase / sentence in response to each question. One-word answers will not be sufficient to gain full marks.

(12 marks)

> Don't try to invent words if you don't know them. If you look at this picture and see a choir (a word that is not on the Edexcel vocabulary list), don't make up a word, express it in a way you know. You could say 'There is a group of students and they are practising a song'.

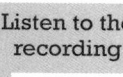

Opinions about school uniform

2 Emilio, Marta and Hugo are talking about school uniform.

   What do they say?

   Listen to the recording and complete the sentences by putting a cross [×] in the correct box for each question.

(a) Emilio thinks …

☐	A	their uniform is very unpopular.
☐	B	all school uniforms should be the same.
☐	C	students should have a say in the uniform colour.

(b) Marta says …

☐	A	all schools ought to have a uniform.
☐	B	buying a uniform is too expensive.
☐	C	they should sell second-hand uniform in schools.

(c) Hugo …

☐	A	says that not having uniform leads to discrimination.
☐	B	worries about families who can't afford the uniform.
☐	C	does not see any connection between uniform and equality.

(3 marks)

> As well as the five minutes of reading time at the start of the exam, there is also a pause after the question number is announced. This gives you a moment to glance over the question again and remind yourself of the scenario and the question style.

My school

Had a go ☐   Nearly there ☐   Nailed it! ☐

Activities in class

Read aloud

1   Emilio, your Chilean friend, tells you about his classes at school.

Read out the text below.

> Me gustan más las clases de educación física porque soy una persona muy activa.
>
> Primero hacemos ejercicio en el gimnasio y luego salimos al campo de deportes para jugar al fútbol o al baloncesto.
>
> No se me da bien la historia porque tenemos que escuchar, leer y escribir todo el tiempo.

Once you have read the text, play the recording and answer two questions related to what you have read.

You are expected to say a few words or a short phrase / sentence in response to each question. One-word answers will not be sufficient to gain full marks.   **(12 marks)**

Remember that the letter *j* and the letter *g* (when followed by *e* or *i*) are pronounced like the 'ch' in the Scottish word 'loch'. (The 'j' sound, like in the English word 'jump', does not exist in Spanish.)

Play the recording to listen to the following words. Repeat the words to practise the sound.   Track 68

dejar, mejor, juntos, jardín

región, alérgico, colegio

general, proteger, gente

A letter about school classes

2   Write a letter to your friend about your classes at school.

You **must** include the following points:

- what your timetable is like
- your opinion of one of your lessons with reasons
- what you did in one of your lessons last week
- what you are going to do in a different class next week.

> Ensure that you don't repeat yourself. The third and fourth bullet points are about class activities, so make sure you talk about different things for each one and don't use the same vocabulary.

Write your answer **in Spanish**. You should aim to write between 80 and 90 words.

....

....

....

....

....

....

....

....

....

....

(18 marks)

Had a go ☐ **Nearly there** ☐ **Nailed it!** ☐

My school

School rules

Dictation

1 You are going to hear someone talking about school rules.

Sentences 1–3: write down the missing words in the gaps provided. In each gap, you will write one word **in Spanish**.

Example: *Hay que respetar al profesor.*

1 Las .... son ....

2 No .... comer ....

3 Tenemos que .... el uniforme ....

Sentences 4–6: write down the full sentences that you hear in the spaces provided, **in Spanish**.

Example: *Nunca llego tarde a las clases.*

4 ....

5 ....

6 .... **(10 marks)**

> If you can understand the sentences, it will help you even more to write the words with the correct spellings. So, use your understanding of the Spanish language to guide you. For instance, after *las* ('the') in the first sentence, the next word must be a feminine plural noun.
>
> You can sometimes use your knowledge of the English language to help. For example, in sentence 5, you will hear the Spanish for 'prohibited'. Your knowledge of the English word will remind you that there is a silent letter 'h' in the Spanish word.

Translation

2 Translate the following five sentences **into Spanish**.

(a) You must do your homework every day.

....

(b) We never arrive late to school.

....

(c) You must not drop litter in the playground.

....

(d) You cannot bring your mobile to class.

....

(e) We must always have the necessary equipment.

....

> When translating 'your homework' or 'your mobile', the best way is to simply use the article (**los** *deberes*, **el** *móvil*). In Spanish it seems obvious that it must be yours, so it isn't felt necessary to say so.
>
> With 'school' and 'class', we leave out the article ('the') in English, but it is always included in Spanish (**el** *instituto / colegio* and **la** *clase*).

(10 marks)

My school

Had a go ☐ Nearly there ☐ Nailed it! ☐

School – the good and the bad

School likes and dislikes

1 Read Nadia's blog about school.

> El sitio que más me gusta en mi colegio es la biblioteca. Tiene muchos ordenadores nuevos.
> Un problema con mi instituto es que no hay igualdad. Por ejemplo, no tenemos un equipo de fútbol para las chicas.

What does she tell us?

Complete the tables **in English**. You do not need to write in full sentences.

> Remember that the questions follow the order of the text. Knowing this helps you locate the correct information in the text.

(a)

The place she likes	....	(1 mark)
The reason she likes it	....	(1 mark)

(b)

The problem she mentions	....	(1 mark)
The example she gives	....	(1 mark)

Translation

2 Translate the following five sentences **into Spanish**.

(a) The head teacher is very strict.

....

(b) I passed the exam last week.

....

(c) We can ask questions in class.

....

(d) Something that I like a lot is the use of technology.

....

(e) Some teachers give us too much homework.

.... (10 marks)

> In the Foundation translation, you can expect all the sentences to be on one topic, four sentences to be in the present tense and one to be in the past tense. The past tense sentence here is sentence (b): the verb *aprobar* (to pass) is regular in the preterite tense.

Had a go ☐ Nearly there ☐ Nailed it! ☐   **My school**

School clubs and activities

A description of a school club

2 Read Indra's account of her favourite school club.

> Cada jueves, en el colegio, voy al Club de Cultura Española que organiza nuestra profesora de castellano*. Dura tres cuartos de hora y cada semana hay un evento diferente. A veces la profesora nos hace una presentación con fotos sobre distintos aspectos del país. Hoy hemos escuchado canciones y disfruté leyendo la letra. De vez en cuando, uno de los estudiantes con más experiencia presenta un proyecto sobre un tema relacionado con España o América Latina. La semana próxima, vamos a probar unas tapas. Todos los estudiantes que participan en el club van a traer algo que han hecho en casa.

castellano – Spanish language

Complete the sentences below.

Put a cross [×] in the correct box for each question.

(a) The club on Thursdays is organised by …
- ☐ A the Cultural Centre.
- ☐ B the language students.
- ☐ C the Spanish teacher.

(b) The sessions last …
- ☐ A an hour.
- ☐ B forty-five minutes.
- ☐ C half an hour.

(c) The teacher tells them …
- ☐ A how to improve their language.
- ☐ B about Spanish music.
- ☐ C different things about the country.

(d) Today in the club, Indra …
- ☐ A enjoyed reading song lyrics.
- ☐ B had fun singing in Spanish.
- ☐ C tried to write a song.

(e) Sometimes, the club is run by …
- ☐ A a visiting speaker.
- ☐ B an older student.
- ☐ C a Spanish-speaking parent.

(f) Next week, they will be …
- ☐ A sampling food.
- ☐ B watching a film.
- ☐ C learning about customs.

(6 marks)

After-school clubs in England and Spain

2 Sofía is talking about after-school clubs in schools. What does she say?

Listen to the recording and answer the following questions **in English**.

You do not need to write in full sentences.

(a) When did Sofía learn about English schools?

.... **(1 mark)**

(b) When did most activities take place?

.... **(1 mark)**

(c) What kind of classes does she say you can attend in Spain? Mention **two**.

.... **(2 marks)**

(d) Why are these activities different from the ones organised in England? Give **two** reasons.

.... **(2 marks)**

My school

Had a go ☐   Nearly there ☐   Nailed it! ☐

Being a good student

A podcast about exams

1 Listen to Hugo's podcast about preparing for exams.

What does he say?

Listen to the recording and put a cross [×] in each one of the **three** correct boxes.

☐	A	You need to make a study plan.
☐	B	Re-reading the text book is the best thing to do.
☐	C	Doing something active is a good study method.
☐	D	Having regular healthy meals is important.
☐	E	Write important dates on paper to stick to your wall.
☐	F	Don't forget to take regular breaks.

(3 marks)

Picture task

See this photo in colour

2 Describe this picture.

Your description **must** cover:
- people
- location
- activity.

> When planning your response to the Picture task, you can take the opportunity to show off a stylish or complex structure that you know. Here, for example, it looks as though the teacher has just asked a question. To say 'has / have just …ed', use *acabar de* in the present tense and add the infinitive.

When you have finished your description, play the recording to hear and respond to two questions relating to the picture.

You are expected to say a few words or a short phrase / sentence in response to each question. One-word answers will not be sufficient to gain full marks.

(12 marks)

68

Had a go ☐ **Nearly there** ☐ **Nailed it!** ☐

My future

Options at 16

Careers Day

1 The head teacher is explaining about Careers Day in the school.

Complete the sentences.

Put a cross [×] in the correct box for each question.

(a) Because of Careers Day, they have cancelled …

☐ **A** all lessons.
☐ **B** Science lessons.
☐ **C** P.E. lessons.

(b) You need to ask the teachers for information if …

☐ **A** you want to take up a new subject.
☐ **B** you are unsure of your grades.
☐ **C** you are thinking of changing schools.

(c) You should go to the library for information on …

☐ **A** university applications.
☐ **B** part-time jobs.
☐ **C** vocational qualifications.

(d) You should go to the technology classroom to hear about …

☐ **A** going to a local college.
☐ **B** chances to study abroad.
☐ **C** work experience opportunities.

(4 marks)

> *Una carrera* can be a career, a university course or a race. It usually depends on the context to make it clear. *Un título* is a qualification, sometimes implying a university qualification or degree.

Read aloud

2 Paula, your Spanish friend, emailed you about her plans for next year.

Read out the text below.

> El año próximo voy a seguir estudiando en el instituto, pero no estoy segura de qué voy a escoger.
> Me gustan las ciencias, y las matemáticas son muy útiles.
> Mi decisión depende de mis notas.

Once you have read the text, play the recording and answer two questions related to what you have read.

You are expected to say a few words or a short phrase / sentence in response to each question. One-word answers will not be sufficient to gain full marks.

(12 marks)

> When you read the word *instituto*, remember that the 't' sound is very pure and not at all like the 'choo' sound we make in English when we say 'insti**tu**te' or '**tu**tor'.
>
> Listen to these words, with the same 'tu' sound being pronounced:
>
> *futuro, aventura, temperatura, instituto*
>
> Track 75

My future

Had a go ☐ Nearly there ☐ Nailed it! ☐

Equality

Comments about discrimination

1 Read these comments from an internet forum on discrimination.

> **Malek:** Yo creo que todavía hay ejemplos donde las mujeres reciben menos dinero por hacer el mismo trabajo que los hombres. Esto pasa a menudo en los medios.
>
> **Carmen:** He oído cosas terribles sobre algunos de los estudiantes en mi instituto simplemente porque sus familias vinieron aquí desde el norte de África.
>
> **Ana:** Algunas chicas tratan mal a mi amiga Karima porque parece un poco diferente. La única diferencia es que lleva un pañuelo sobre el pelo. Es una costumbre entre las personas de su fe.

Who says what? Choose the correct answers.

Put a cross [×] in the correct column for each question.

	Who talks about …	Malek	Carmen	Ana
(a)	… discrimination in school?			
(b)	… religious discrimination?			
(c)	… pay inequality?			
(d)	… racial discrimination?			
(e)	… gender discrimination?			
(f)	… discrimination because of clothing?			

(1 mark) each

> There is some less common vocabulary in the comments above, so read them with care. If you get stuck, move on to the next question – you may arrive at an answer because you have eliminated other possibilities, but that's fine!

Translation

2 Translate this passage **into Spanish**.

> Our new head teacher has improved many of the facilities in the school in order to create a better experience for disabled people. We now have a lift that can take wheelchairs up to the first floor. If, for some reason, they cannot attend class, they can take part from home on their laptop.

....
....
....
....
....

(10 marks)

> The word order for 'we now have' should be 'now we have' in Spanish. For 'take up' you can use *llevar* or *subir*. For 'from home' you would say 'from their house'.

70

Had a go ☐ Nearly there ☐ Nailed it! ☐

My future

Future study plans

A college visit

1 Natalia and Juan are talking about the college they are visiting.

What do they like and dislike about it?

Listen to the recording and complete the following tables **in English**.

You do not need to write in full sentences.

(a) Natalia

likes …	…………………………………………………………………………………………	(1 mark)
dislikes …	…………………………………………………………………………………………	(1 mark)

(b) Juan

likes …	…………………………………………………………………………………………	(1 mark)
dislikes …	…………………………………………………………………………………………	(1 mark)

> The information you need for the answers comes in the same order as the questions. So you will first hear Natalia speak; she will start by mentioning what she likes and will then talk about what she does not like. The same will then happen with Juan.

General conversation

2 After the Picture task in the exam, you won't see the general conversation questions written down; you will only hear your teacher asking them.

Here are some typical questions on the topic of future study plans. Think about how you would answer them. Then play the recording of the questions and pause the recording after each question to give your answer.

- ¿Qué planes tienes para tus estudios el año próximo?
- ¿Cuáles son tus razones por escoger este curso?
- ¿Quieres ir a la universidad?
- ¿Cuáles son los beneficios de ir a la universidad?
- ¿Cuáles son los aspectos negativos?
- ¿Qué otras cosas te gustaría aprender en el futuro?

(16 marks)

> Remember what examiners are looking for in order to award in the top band of marks. Your answers should be easily comprehensible and relevant to the questions. Your ideas should be developed through extended sequences of speech, you should aim for a wide and accurate range of vocabulary and grammar, and you should include references to the past, present and future.

My future

Had a go ☐ Nearly there ☐ Nailed it! ☐

Future plans

Dictation

1 You are going to hear someone talking about future plans.

Sentences 1–2: write down the missing words in the gaps provided. In each gap, you will write one word **in Spanish**.

Example: <u>Tendré</u> muchos <u>amigos</u> cuando <u>vaya</u> a la universidad.

1 Voy a .... una ....

2 Me gustaría .... a otra ....

Sentences 3–6: write down the full sentences that you hear in the spaces provided, **in Spanish**.

Example: <u>Algún día voy a vivir en el extranjero.</u>

3 ....
4 ....
5 ....
6 ....

(10 marks)

> Words like *farmacia* are not stressed on the letter *i*, so there is no accent on the *i*. In words like *sería* (in the conditional tense) the letter *i* is stressed, therefore an accent is needed. Try to apply this rule to the four words in this category in the Dictation.

A blog about studies and future plans

2 Write a blog about your studies and future plans.

You **must** mention the following points:
- your current studies
- the pros and cons of going to university
- what you wanted to be when you were little
- your future plans.

> For the third bullet point, you will be talking about what you <u>used to</u> want to be when <u>you were</u> little, so you will need the imperfect tense for these verbs.

Write your answer **in Spanish**. You should aim to write between 130 and 150 words.

....
....
....
....
....
....
....
....
....
....

(22 marks)

Had a go ☐   Nearly there ☐   Nailed it! ☐   **My future**

Part-time jobs and money

A new job

1 Julia is about to start a new part-time job.

What does she say about it?

Listen to the recording and complete the following tables **in English**.

You do not need to write in full sentences.

(a)
The day she will work
....

(1 mark)

(b)
Where in the supermarket she will work
....

(1 mark)

(c)
The time she must go in tomorrow
....

(1 mark)

> In questions (a) and (c) you need to listen carefully as you will hear two possible answers (e.g. two different days and two different times). You need to pay close attention in order to eliminate the wrong answer and select the correct one.

Picture task

See this photo in colour

2 Describe the photo. Write four short sentences **in Spanish**.

.... (2 marks)

.... (2 marks)

.... (2 marks)

.... (2 marks)

> This is the first question on the Foundation Writing paper, allowing you to give straightforward pieces of information about any aspect of the photo. Your sentences just need to be relevant to the photo and communicate a clear message.

Opinions about jobs

My future — Had a go ☐ Nearly there ☐ Nailed it! ☐

A job forum

Target grade 2

1 Read the comments and queries on an internet forum.

> **Pilar:** Me gustaría ser profesora de niños pequeños. ¿Cuántos años de formación tienes que hacer?
>
> **Andrea:** Me interesa trabajar como policía en el futuro. ¿Me puedes decir cuál es el salario?
>
> **Marcos:** Quisiera ganarme la vida como escritor. ¿Qué asignatura sería mejor estudiar en la universidad?

Who asks about what? Choose the correct answers.

Put a cross [×] in the correct column for each question.

	Who asks about …	Pilar	Andrea	Marcos	
(a)	… being a writer?				(1 mark)
(b)	… choosing a subject?				(1 mark)
(c)	… joining the police?				(1 mark)
(d)	… becoming a teacher?				(1 mark)
(e)	… doing training?				(1 mark)
(f)	… the money you earn?				(1 mark)

Target grade 4–9

Read aloud

2 Monika, your Spanish friend, writes about her ideas for possible jobs.

Read out the text below.

> Creo que me gustaría ser actriz, pero sé que es muy difícil encontrar empleo en el cine o la televisión. Sin embargo, hay que seguir los sueños. Me gustaría mucho ir a la universidad para estudiar drama y teatro. Así, tendré un título si no logro mi objetivo.

> Be careful when pronouncing *i* and *e*. The letter *i* is always pronounced as in *si* or *ir* so it will be the same in *ideal* – do not be tempted to produce the sound 'eye' like in the English word 'ideal'.
>
> You should also hear the difference in the way you pronounce *mi* and *me*, so when you say *me gustaría*, ensure you say *me* (meh) and not *mi*.
>
> Listen to these examples: *idea, ideal, final, dieta, me gustaría, me llamo, mi casa, mi familia*

Track 80

Listen to the recording

Once you have read the text, play the recording and answer two questions related to what you have read.

You are expected to say a few words or a short phrase / sentence in response to each question. One-word answers will not be sufficient to gain full marks. **(12 marks)**

You can a sample recording of the text, questions and answers in the Answers section.

Had a go ☐ **Nearly there** ☐ **Nailed it!** ☐   **My future**

Pros and cons of different jobs

Picture task

1 Describe this picture.

Your description **must** cover:
- people
- location
- activity.

When you have finished your description, play the recording to hear and respond to two questions relating to the picture.

You are expected to say a few words or a short phrase / sentence in response to each question. One-word answers will not be sufficient to gain full marks.

(12 marks)

> With this picture you could guess that it is the start of the day, perhaps nine o'clock because the people are arriving in the office or have just arrived (using *acabar de* + infinitive). You could also consider why the man has brought his bike into the office (to keep it safe? – *para mantenerla segura*).

Translation

2 Translate the following sentences **into English**.

(a) Quiero trabajar en una oficina con equipo moderno.

....

(b) Hay muchas reglas en esta empresa.

....

(c) Paula espera ser científica o profesora.

....

(d) Fui al extranjero seis veces cuando trabajaba con la compañía.

....

(e) No me gustaría ser médico, es demasiada responsabilidad.

....

(10 marks)

> Be careful with words that have more than one meaning. Think about which meaning makes sense in the context. For example, *equipo* can mean 'team' or 'equipment' and *regla* can mean 'rule' or 'ruler'.

My future

Had a go ☐ Nearly there ☐ Nailed it! ☐

Job adverts, skills needed

Translation

1 Translate the following five sentences **into Spanish**.

(a) I need to call the company.

....

(b) I am hard-working and I have a positive attitude.

....

(c) I am looking for information online.

....

(d) My sister found a job in the newspaper.

....

(e) The firm wants people with experience.

.... **(10 marks)**

> Remember that 'to look for' is *buscar* – you do not need an extra word for 'for'. Also, in sentence (c) you can use the ordinary present (*busco*) or the present continuous (*estoy buscando*).

Listen to the recording

Role play

2 **Setting: An interview for a summer job on a campsite**

Scenario:
- You are being interviewed for a summer job on a Spanish campsite.
- Play the recording to hear the teacher's role.
- You will hear questions **in Spanish** and you must answer **in Spanish** in the pauses.
- You are expected to say a few words or a short phrase / sentence in response to each prompt. One-word answers will not be sufficient to gain full marks.

Task:
1 Say what sort of person you are.
2 Say why you would like the job.
3 Say when you can start work.
4 Ask a question about the hours.
5 Ask a question about the pay.

(10 marks)

> There are all sorts of reasons why you might want the job: to gain work experience, to practise your Spanish, because you love spending time in Spain and, of course, to earn some money.

Had a go ☐   Nearly there ☐   Nailed it! ☐   **My future**

Applying for jobs

A job advertisement

1 Marcos is talking about a job he has seen advertised.

What does he say?

Listen to the recording and complete the sentences by putting a cross [×] in the correct box for each question.

(a) The job is in a …

☐ **A** department store.
☐ **B** menswear shop.
☐ **C** shoe shop.

(b) They need someone to work …

☐ **A** full time.
☐ **B** afternoons only.
☐ **C** Saturdays.

(c) The advert specifies that …

☐ **A** sales experience is essential.
☐ **B** some experience is preferable.
☐ **C** no experience is necessary.

(3 marks)

Dictation

2 You are going to hear someone talking about applying for jobs.

Sentences 1–3: write down the missing words in the gaps provided. In each gap, you will write one word **in Spanish**.

Example: *El <u>salario</u> es muy <u>bajo</u>.*

1 Voy a ……………………………… a este ……………………………………………… .

2 Mi ……………………………… es ……………………………………………………… .

3 Tus ……………………………… parecen muy ……………………………………… .

Sentences 4–6: write down the full sentences that you hear in the spaces provided, **in Spanish**.

Example: *<u>Empiezo a trabajar la próxima semana.</u>*

4 ………………………………………………………………………………………………… .

5 ………………………………………………………………………………………………… .

6 ………………………………………………………………………………………………… .

(10 marks)

My future

Had a go ☐ Nearly there ☐ Nailed it! ☐

Preparing for interviews

Picture task

1 Describe this picture.

Your description **must** cover:
- people
- location
- activity.

See this photo in colour

> With this picture, you will want to mention what the people are looking at. One man is looking at his watch (*el reloj*) but, with the others, you need to use your imagination. They could be looking at information about the company, ideas they have for the interview, details and figures (*detalles y cifras*), things they want to say or a presentation they have to give.

Listen to the recording

When you have finished your description, play the recording to hear and respond to two questions relating to the picture.

You are expected to say a few words or a short phrase / sentence in response to each question. One-word answers will not be sufficient to gain full marks.

(12 marks)

Translation

2 Translate the passage **into English**.

> Ayer fui a la oficina de turismo para una entrevista. Llevé un traje gris, una camisa blanca y una corbata roja. Me sentía bastante nervioso pero el jefe era muy simpático y cuando me hizo preguntas pude contestar con confianza. Al final, me dijo que me llamarían este jueves para decirme si he tenido éxito.

....
....
....
....
....
....
....
....

(10 marks)

> Although *hacer* usually means 'to do' or 'to make', in the context of *hacer preguntas* it cannot mean either of these two verbs, because you do not do or make questions. In this case, you must remember that when *hacer* is with *preguntas*, it is translated as 'to ask' (questions).

Had a go ☐ **Nearly there** ☐ **Nailed it!** ☐

My future

Working to help others

Helping others

1 Emilio, Nadia and Malek are talking about what they do to help others.

Listen to the recording and complete the following tables **in English**.

You do not need to write in full sentences.

(a)
The work that Emilio does
....

(1 mark)

(b)
The work that Nadia does
....

(1 mark)

(c)
The place where Malek works
....

(1 mark)

> You cannot offer two answers. For example, if you are unsure what Nadia does because you can't decide whether she cares for her neighbour or does the neighbour's gardening, do not write both – you will not receive a mark. You must choose between the two, and then at least you have a 50 / 50 chance of being right.

Picture task

2 Describe the photo. Write four short sentences **in Spanish**.

.... (2 marks)

.... (2 marks)

.... (2 marks)

.... (2 marks)

My future

Had a go ☐ Nearly there ☐ Nailed it! ☐

Equality and helping others

Changing attitudes

1 Read this report about changing attitudes.

> Actualmente las personas con discapacidad reciben más atención que antes. Creo que los Juegos Paralímpicos han ayudado mucho para dar este paso* positivo. También creo que hay más igualdad de oportunidades en los medios. Una actriz en una silla de ruedas es una de las estrellas de una serie muy popular entre los jóvenes.

paso – step

Put a cross [×] next to each one of the **three** correct statements.

☐	A	People with disabilities are more visible these days.
☐	B	The world of sport has had a positive influence.
☐	C	In some areas, facilities are inadequate.
☐	D	Some companies seek to employ more people with a disability.
☐	E	There is greater equality in the media these days.
☐	F	An actor in a wheelchair has complained about discrimination.

(3 marks)

> The Reading paper is the only exam where words that are not on the prescribed list may be seen. These words will either be glossed with an asterisk and explained below (like *paso* in this text), be part of a question where you have to work out the meaning, or be so similar to the English word that their meaning is obvious (like *Paralímpicos* in this text).

Picture task

See this photo in colour

> With this photo, you can talk about the sport they have played, what they are wearing and the fact that it is a competition in a stadium with lots of people watching. It is difficult to know who won the match and you can always say that: *No es posible saber quién ganó el partido*, or *No sabemos quién ganó el partido*.

1 Describe this picture.

Your description **must** cover:
- people
- location
- activity.

Listen to the recording

When you have finished your description, play the recording to hear and respond to two questions relating to the picture.

You are expected to say a few words or a short phrase / sentence in response to each question. One-word answers will not be sufficient to gain full marks.

(12 marks)

Had a go ☐ Nearly there ☐ Nailed it! ☐

Environment

The environment and me

A letter about the environment

1 Write a letter to your friend about helping the environment.

You **must** include the following points:
- how you travel to school
- your opinion of public transport in your area with reasons
- what you did to help the environment last week
- what you are going to do in the future to save energy.

> In the Writing paper, the aim is to show off your Spanish so don't worry if you have to bend the truth a little in order to complete the task. Use the vocabulary you know and adapt it to the task as required.

Write your answer **in Spanish**. You should aim to write between 80 and 90 words.

....
....
....
....
....
....
....
....
....
....
....

(18 marks)

Translation

2 Translate the paragraph **into Spanish**.

> It is very important to protect the planet and to do what we can to care for the environment. In our house, we usually recycle paper, bottles and plastic. When I went out last week, I used public transport. My sister is going to take her used clothes to a second-hand shop.

> When 'what?' is a question, use *¿qué?*
>
> When 'what' is not a question (as in 'what we can' in the first sentence of the translation), use *lo que*.
>
> To translate 'second-hand shop', be careful with the word order. It will be 'shop of second-hand', and remember that *mano* is feminine.

....
....
....
....
....
....
....

(10 marks)

Environment

Had a go ☐ Nearly there ☐ Nailed it! ☐

Local environmental issues

Picture task

See this photo in colour

1. Describe this picture.

   Your description **must** cover:
   - people
   - location
   - activity.

   > In this picture you can talk about the team or group of eight young people who are working to help to care for the environment. You could talk about the blue T-shirt they all wear, the action of picking up rubbish and where they are – perhaps a park in the city. Don't forget the weather and even your opinion of what they are doing.

Listen to the recording

When you have finished your description, play the recording to hear and respond to two questions relating to the picture.

You are expected to say a few words or a short phrase / sentence in response to each question. One-word answers will not be sufficient to gain full marks. **(12 marks)**

Translation

2. Translate the following five sentences **into Spanish**.

   (a) There is a lot of pollution in the sea.

   ....

   (b) I like the green spaces in the city.

   ....

   (c) We are going to walk to town.

   ....

   (d) My mother hated the noise from the road.

   ....

   (e) The air is cleaner in the countryside.

   ....

> To create the comparative adjective 'cleaner than', you need to say 'more clean than'. 'Clean' still agrees with its noun ('air'), and the verb to use with 'clean' is *estar*.

(10 marks)

Had a go ☐ Nearly there ☐ Nailed it! ☐   **Environment**

Global environmental issues

An environmental issue

1 Julia and Miguel are taking about an environmental issue.

What do they say?

Listen to the recording and complete the sentences by putting a cross [×] in the correct box for each question.

(a) Miguel asks if Julia has heard about the …

☐ **A** fire.
☐ **B** flood.
☐ **C** accident.

(b) Julia says that many people …

☐ **A** are without power.
☐ **B** are stranded.
☐ **C** are homeless.

(c) Miguel says that …

☐ **A** no one was killed.
☐ **B** many are injured.
☐ **C** people are missing.

(3 marks)

> Remember that you will hear the Listening recordings three times. Try to just listen the first time. You can make notes immediately afterwards, but concentrating on listening intently will ensure you grasp the gist of the recording and alert you to the important bits of the conversation.

Dictation

2 You are going to hear someone talking about the environment.

Sentences 1–2: write down the missing words in the gaps provided. In each gap, you will write one word **in Spanish**.

Example: *En mi país, hay crisis en el campo.*

1 .... usar menos .... para la ....

2 Siguen .... muchos .... en la ....

Sentences 3–6: write down the full sentences that you hear in the spaces provided, **in Spanish**.

Example: *El cambio climático está causando muchos problemas.*

3 ....
4 ....
5 ....
6 ....

(10 marks)

> Remember that the sound 'kwa' is always spelt *cua* in Spanish (as in *cuatro*) and never 'qua' as in English. Also, if you hear what sounds like 'tha' (with a soft 'th' as in 'Na**th**an') it will be *za* in Spanish. The combination of letters t + h does not exist in Spanish.

Environment

Had a go ☐ Nearly there ☐ Nailed it! ☐

Caring for the planet

Comments about the environment

1 Read these comments on the environment from an internet forum.

> **Andrea:** Mañana voy a estar con un grupo de ciudadanos que está enfadado. Nos vamos a manifestar contra la falta de acción del gobierno en el tema de la polución del aire de la ciudad.
>
> **Carla:** Me preocupa mucho que los presidentes del mundo no hagan lo suficiente para resolver el problema del cambio climático. Si las temperaturas siguen subiendo, vamos a tener condiciones que amenazan la vida de la gente.
>
> **Raúl:** Quiero dar las gracias al grupo de jóvenes que se ofreció a limpiar el río. Ahora las aguas están puras y sanas y he visto la vuelta de los pájaros y peces a la zona.

Who says what? Choose the correct answers.

Put a cross [×] in the correct column for each question.

	Who …	Andrea	Carla	Raúl
(a)	… is grateful to a band of volunteers?			
(b)	… feels that world leaders are not doing enough?			
(c)	… is going to take part in a protest march?			
(d)	… has seen nature return to a once-polluted area?			
(e)	… is concerned about breathing contaminated air?			
(f)	… believes the changing climate is a threat to life?			

(6 marks)

> When you answer question (b), you may notice that both Andrea and Carla complain about the authorities not taking enough action. However, only one of them is talking about world presidents; the other is talking about government.

Read aloud

2 Amira, your Chilean friend, has written about the environment where she lives.

Read out the text below.

> La zona donde vivo no sufre problemas de polución.
> Aquí en las montañas el aire es puro y tenemos una gran cantidad de especies de animales y pájaros.
> Pero, abajo en el valle, han cortado muchos árboles. En la ciudad se nota el humo y el ruido de la industria.

> Remember that the letter *h* is not pronounced at all. You should not hear the slightest breath at the beginning of words like *han* and *humo*. Pretend that the *h* is not even there.

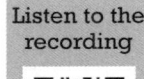

Listen to the recording

Once you have read the text, play the recording and answer two questions related to what you have read.

You are expected to say a few words or a short phrase / sentence in response to each question. One-word answers will not be sufficient to gain full marks.

(12 marks)

Had a go ☐   **Nearly there** ☐   **Nailed it!** ☐

Environment

A greener future

Picture task

1. Describe this picture.

   Your description **must** cover:
   - people
   - location
   - activity.

See this photo in colour

When you have finished your description, play the recording to hear and respond to two questions relating to the picture.

You are expected to say a few words or a short phrase / sentence in response to each question. One-word answers will not be sufficient to gain full marks. **(12 marks)**

> These children could be in a park (*un parque*) or in the countryside (*el campo*). They could be studying nature (*la naturaleza*) or learning about trees and flowers (*árboles y flores*). It could be a class of pupils who are doing a competition (*una competición*) about the natural world (*el mundo natural*).

Translation

2. Translate the paragraph **into Spanish**.

> I believe that the government ought to spend more on the development of renewable resources. The sun, the wind and the sea have a lot of power and we will be able to use it to create energy. Also, it is clean energy that causes less pollution. I read this information online.

....
....
....
....
....
....
.... **(10 marks)**

> To translate 'we will be able', you use the future tense of the verb *poder*. Remember that it has an irregular stem in the future: it loses an 'e'. Normally, the future endings are added to the infinitive, but some verbs lose the 'e' of the infinitive ending, like *poder* (*podr*…), *saber* (*sabr*…) and *querer* (*querr*…)

About the exams

Had a go ☐ Nearly there ☐ Nailed it! ☐

Practice for Paper 1: Speaking

Practise for the Speaking tasks with this selection of exam-style questions.

Read aloud

1 Your friend Ana has written about the environment.

   Read out the text below.

   > En mi ciudad el aire no está muy limpio porque hay mucha polución de los coches.
   > También se puede ver papeles en las calles.
   > El medio ambiente es mejor en otoño cuando hace menos calor.

   When you get a and i together, as in aire, they do not sound like the English word 'air'. They sound like a combination of 'a' and 'i' and make a sound like 'eye'.

Track 94

Once you have read the text, play the recording and answer two questions related to what you have read.

You are expected to say a few words or a short phrase / sentence in response to each question. One-word answers will not be sufficient to gain full marks.

You can hear a sample recording of the text, questions and answers in the Answers section.

(12 marks)

Read aloud

2 Your friend Raúl has written about himself and his family.

   Read out the text below.

   > Soy hijo único y vivo en una ciudad en el oeste de España. Mi padre es policía y mi madre es jefa de ventas en una compañía de seguridad. Los dos tienen cuarenta y cinco años. Generalmente, me llevo muy bien con ellos porque tenemos el mismo sentido del humor.

   Remember that if a word has an accent, that is where the word should be stressed: único / policía / compañía.

Track 95

Once you have read the text, play the recording and answer two questions related to what you have read.

You are expected to say a few words or a short phrase / sentence in response to each question. One-word answers will not be sufficient to gain full marks.

You can hear a sample recording of the text, questions and answers in the Answers section.

(12 marks)

86

Had a go ☐ Nearly there ☐ Nailed it! ☐   **About the exams**

Practice for Paper 1: Speaking

Practise for the Speaking tasks with this selection of exam-style questions.

Role play

Track 96

1 **Setting: At a leisure centre**

   Scenario:
   - You are at a leisure centre, and you are talking to an employee about your family using the swimming pool.
   - Play the recording to hear the teacher's role.
   - You will hear questions **in Spanish** and you must answer **in Spanish** in the pauses.
   - You are expected to say a few words or a short phrase / sentence in response to each prompt. One-word answers will not be sufficient to gain full marks.

   Task:
   1 Ask a question about the price.
   2 Say who wants to use the pool.
   3 Say what other sports you like.
   4 Say where you are staying.
   5 Ask a question about opening times.

   (10 marks)

   Questions about time will start with *¿A qué hora ...?* and you can then use *se abre* or *está abierto/a* + the name of the place.

   You can hear a sample of the full role play in the Answers section.

Picture task

2 Describe this picture.

   Your description **must** cover:
   - people
   - location
   - activity.

   You could mention clean sand, calm sea, hot weather, blue sky, and buildings in the distance as well as the people, location and activity.

See this photo in colour

Track 97

When you have finished your description, play the recording to hear and respond to two questions relating to the picture.

You are expected to say a few words or a short phrase / sentence in response to each question. One-word answers will not be sufficient to gain full marks.

(12 marks)

87

Practice for Paper 2: Listening

Had a go ☐   Nearly there ☐   Nailed it! ☐

About the exams

Practise for the Listening tasks with this selection of exam-style questions.

Target grade 2

Track 98

Eating out

1. Amira is talking about a meal she had in a restaurant.

   What does she say?

   Listen to the recording and complete the sentences by putting a cross [×] in the correct box for each question.

   (a) Amira thought the vegetarian food ...

   ☐ A had too much salt.
   ☐ B was very tasty.
   ☐ C was a bit boring.

   (b) Amira did not like ...

   ☐ A the bread.
   ☐ B the fish.
   ☐ C the meat.

   (2 marks)

Target grade 3

Track 99

TV programmes

2. David is talking about what he watches on TV.

   What types of programmes does he mention?

   Listen to the recording and put a cross [×] in each one of the **three** correct boxes.

   ☐ A music
   ☐ B sport
   ☐ C history
   ☐ D films
   ☐ E cooking
   ☐ F travel

   > You can use the space to the right of the grid to tick any words that you hear while you are listening. A quick tick will not stop you listening to the recording. Remember to mark your final answers in the boxes with a cross.

   (3 marks)

Target grade 5

Track 100

A festival

3. Natalia is talking in a podcast.

   What does she say about the festival?

   > This is a 'process' question. Listen to all of the recording; don't jump to conclusions on the basis of one word.

   Complete the gap in each sentence using a word or phrase from the box below. There are more words / phrases than gaps.

park	square	port	high street
2nd	5th	15th	

   (a) Most events this year will be in the .... **(1 mark)**

   (b) Children's games are in the .... **(1 mark)**

   (c) The main events are on the .... **(1 mark)**

Had a go ☐ Nearly there ☐ Nailed it! ☐   **About the exams**

Practice for Paper 2: Listening

Practise for the Listening tasks with this selection of exam-style questions.

Studying

1 Sofía and Nadim are talking about their studies.

What do they like and dislike about them?

Listen to the recording and complete the following tables in English.

You do not need to write in full sentences.

The challenge is to keep your answers brief but ensure you give the necessary details.

(a) Sofía

likes …	....	(1 mark)
dislikes …	....	(1 mark)

(b) Nadim

likes …	....	(1 mark)
dislikes …	....	(1 mark)

Dictation

2 You are going to hear someone talking about issues of equality.

Sentences 1–2: write down the missing words in the gaps provided. In each gap, you will write one word **in Spanish**.

Example: En mi <u>escuela</u> ayudamos a los <u>alumnos</u> con <u>discapacidad</u>.

1 Faltan .... para las .... de ....

2 Hay que .... un .... cerca de la ....

Sentences 3–6: write down the full sentences that you hear in the spaces provided, **in Spanish**.

Example: <u>La igualdad de género es muy importante.</u>

3 ....

4 ....

5 ....

6 ....

(10 marks)

Remember that the three words that are not from the prescribed list come in sentences 1 and 2.

About the exams

Had a go ☐   Nearly there ☐   Nailed it! ☐

Practice for Paper 3: Reading

Practise for the Reading tasks with this selection of exam-style questions.

Target grade 3-4

Food and drink

1 Read these online restaurant reviews.

> **Carla:** Fuimos a un restaurante para celebrar el cumpleaños de mi madre. Nos gustó mucho toda la comida y pasamos una tarde muy buena.
>
> **Daniel:** Había una oferta especial cuando fuimos y la comida fue bastante barata, pero nos sirvieron el café frío al final de la cena.
>
> **Monika:** Tienen una lista de entrantes muy ricos. Por otra parte, los postres no son muy interesantes, helado o fruta y poco más.

Who says what? Choose the correct answers.

Put a cross [×] in the correct column for each question.

	Who …	Carla	Daniel	Monika	
(a)	… thought the starters were great?				(1 mark)
(b)	… was there for a family event?				(1 mark)
(c)	… found the desserts disappointing?				(1 mark)
(d)	… enjoyed all the food?				(1 mark)
(e)	… thought the price was reasonable?				(1 mark)
(f)	… was served a cold drink?				(1 mark)

> It often helps to read the options first, so you know what to look out for when you read the text.

Places in town

2 Read Manuel's text message.

> Recuerda que mañana es un día de fiesta y el supermercado estará cerrado. Si necesitas ir de compras, debes ir hoy. El sábado hay una exposición de cuadros famosos en el pueblo. Si te interesa ir, podemos verla juntos e ir de tapas después. ¿Qué te parece?

Complete the sentences below. Put a cross [×] in the correct box for each question.

(a) You should go shopping …

☐	**A** today.
☐	**B** tomorrow.
☐	**C** on Saturday.

(1 mark)

(b) He recommends going to …

☐	**A** a parade in town.
☐	**B** a celebrity football match.
☐	**C** an art exhibition.

(1 mark)

(c) Afterwards, he suggests …

☐	**A** seeing a film.
☐	**B** eating out.
☐	**C** going for a drink.

(1 mark)

Had a go ☐   Nearly there ☐   Nailed it! ☐

About the exams

Practice for Paper 3: Reading

Practise for the Reading tasks with this selection of exam-style questions.

Future opportunities

1 Read this extract from a webpage about voluntary work on a farm in South America.

> **Trabajo A:** Trabajar con animales – aprenderás a cuidar de los caballos y a darles de comer. Por las tardes, podrás ayudar en las clases cuando los niños vienen a aprender a montar a caballo.
>
> **Trabajo B:** Trabajar en una granja* – tenemos unas cuarenta vacas en nuestros campos y usando la leche de estas *vacas*, aprenderás a hacer queso y yogur. De vez en cuando, estarás en la tienda vendiendo los productos que has ayudado a preparar.
>
> **Trabajo C:** Trabajar con turistas – por la mañana estarás con la gente que visita la granja explicando el trabajo que hacemos. Por la tarde los acompañarás en una excursión y explicarás la historia de la región.

*granja – farm

Complete the tables **in English**. You do not need to write in full sentences.

(a) Job A

| One thing you learn | .... | (1 mark) |
| Afternoon task | .... | (1 mark) |

(b) Job B

| Main job | .... | (1 mark) |
| Other task | .... | (1 mark) |

(c) Job C

| Role in mornings | .... | (1 mark) |
| Role during the trip | .... | (1 mark) |

(d) Which of these is the best translation for the word *vacas*?

Put a cross [×] in the correct box.

☐ **A** crops   ☐ **B** cows   ☐ **C** chickens   (1 mark)

Translation: My job

2 Translate the following paragraph **into English**.

> Soy jefa de un grupo de personas que trabajan conmigo en la oficina de ventas de una gran empresa. Ayer había una reunión con los otros jefes y, varias veces, uno de ellos empezó a hablar mientras yo estaba hablando. Piensa que su opinión es más importante que la mía. Me molesta mucho.

....
....
....
....
....

(10 marks)

About the exams

Had a go ☐ Nearly there ☐ Nailed it! ☐

Practice for Paper 4: Writing

Practise for the Writing tasks with this selection of exam-style questions.

Picture task

1 Describe the photo. Write four short sentences **in Spanish**.

See this photo in colour

.... (2 marks)
.... (2 marks)
.... (2 marks)
.... (2 marks)

An article about shopping

2 Write an article about shopping.

You **must** include the following points:
- what you like to buy
- your opinion of the shops in your town / village
- when you will next go shopping.

> You can give your opinion using phrases like *Me gusta ...*, *Me encanta ...*, *Odio ...* or adjectives like *bonito/a*, *excelente*, *interesante*, *terrible*, *maravilloso/a*.

Write your answer **in Spanish**. You should aim to write between 40 and 50 words.

....
....
....
....
....
.... (14 marks)

Translation: Travel

3 Translate the following five sentences **into Spanish**.

(a) There are lots of cars in the city.
....

(b) The airport is not very far.
....

(c) We want to hire bikes this afternoon.
....

(d) I have my passport and our tickets.
....

(e) I went to the island by boat yesterday.
.... (10 marks)

> Remember that when you are describing where something is (e.g. the airport) you need the verb *estar* for 'to be'.

Had a go ☐ Nearly there ☐ Nailed it! ☐

About the exams

Practice for Paper 4: Writing

Practise for the Writing tasks with this selection of exam-style questions.

A blog about friendship

1 Write a blog about friends and friendship.

You **must** include the following points:
- what makes a good friend
- your best friend's good and bad points
- something you did to help a friend
- what activities you will do with friends during the holidays.

Write your answer **in Spanish**. You should aim to write between 130 and 150 words.

If you run out of space, continue your answer on your own paper.

....

....

....

....

....

....

....

....

....

....

....

....

(22 marks)

Translation: A healthy lifestyle

2 Translate the following paragraph **into Spanish**.

> To have a healthy lifestyle, it is important to do exercise and to eat a variety of different foods. However, you also need to rest and to sleep well. Having hobbies is a good way of relaxing. Yesterday I read a magazine and I played tennis. My brother won the match.

....

....

....

....

(10 marks)

> The translation starts with 'To have', which is another way of saying 'In order to have'. When the phrase 'in order to' is implied, you will need the word *para* in Spanish. For the sentence that starts with 'Having', you need a simple infinitive. In total there are seven infinitives in this translation!

Grammar

Had a go ☐   Nearly there ☐   Nailed it! ☐

Nouns and articles

> Remember not all words ending in *a* are feminine or ending in *o* are masculine! There are exceptions.

1 Write the correct definite article: *el, la, los, las*.

Example: la gente

(a) .... mesa
(b) .... fútbol
(c) .... patatas fritas
(d) .... dientes
(e) .... mano
(f) .... piso
(g) .... ciencias
(h) .... entrantes
(i) .... problema
(j) .... foto

2 Complete the sentences with either the definite article *el, la, los, las* or the indefinite article *un, una*. Remember to think about gender and whether it is singular or plural.

Example: En casa tengo un perro que es negro y blanco.

(a) En mi opinión, las hamburguesas son más ricas que .... tortillas.
(b) En mi casa hay .... cuarto de baño y tres dormitorios.
(c) No me gusta .... inglés porque es complicado.
(d) Todos .... martes tengo club de baile.
(e) En la mesa hay .... regla y tres bolígrafos.
(f) Mi instituto es grande y hay .... campo de deportes.
(g) Me he roto .... pie y me duele mucho.
(h) .... domingo fuimos a una piscina al aire libre cerca de mi casa.

> Often we use articles in English when in Spanish they are not needed, for example when talking about jobs, and after *sin* and *con*. Sometimes we use articles in Spanish when we would not in English, for example when talking generally (noun at the start of a sentence), expressing opinions, before the days of the week (*el lunes voy a …*).

3 Read the sentences and cross out any articles that have been used where they are not needed.

Example: No tengo ~~un~~ coche porque prefiero viajar en metro.

(a) Vivo en un piso cómodo en las afueras.
(b) Mi padre es un policía y mi madre es una médica.
(c) Hay muy pocos estudiantes en el instituto sin un móvil.
(d) Escribo con un bolígrafo en mi clase de …
(e) En el futuro me gustaría ser una actriz.
(f) El deporte es muy importante para llevar una vida sana.
(g) Odio las clases de música porque no puedo cantar bien.
(h) Se puede reservar dos habitaciones con una ducha.

Had a go ☐ Nearly there ☐ Nailed it! ☐

Grammar

Adjectives

> Most adjectives agree as follows: end in **-o**: *alto / alta / altos / altas*
> end in **-e**: add **-s** in the plural
> end in **consonant***: add **-es** in the plural
> *Nationalities also have a separate feminine singular form: *española*

1 Find the correct adjective from the list. Remember that as well as making sense, the adjective must agree with the noun.

   Example: una mujer seria

   (a) una cama ....
   (b) dos gatos ....
   (c) un vestido ....
   (d) las películas son ....
   (e) el profesor es ....
   (f) las actrices son ....
   (g) la playa es ....
   (h) nuestros coches son ....

   cómoda
   baratos
   español
   interesantes
   bonita
   rojo
   seria
   simpáticas
   contentos

2 Choose the correct adjective.

   Example: Vivo en un piso muy *pequeña* / (*pequeño*) / *pequeños*.

   (a) Me quedé en un hotel *moderno / moderna / modernos* de cuatro estrellas.
   (b) Me gusta llevar pantalones *cómodas / cómodos / cómodo*.
   (c) Creo que mi instituto es bastante *bueno / buen / buena*.
   (d) La información era *importantes / importante / importan*.
   (e) La estación está siempre *limpia / limpio / limpias*.
   (f) Me encantan las ciencias porque son muy *útiles / útil / utilizas*.

   > Some adjectives have shortened forms which are positioned before the noun:
   > *un coche bueno* → *un buen coche*

3 Write out these sentences with the correct adjective in the correct place.

   Example: Suelo comer fruta porque es sana y rica. (mucho / mucha)
              Suelo comer *mucha* fruta porque es sana y rica.

   (a) En Inglaterra hay gente que habla muy bien castellano. (poco / poca)

   ....

   (b) Lo mejor es que tiene un jardín. (bonito / bonita)

   ....

   (c) Estamos porque hace buen tiempo. (contento / contentas)

   ....

   (d) En el futuro habrá una estación en las afueras de la ciudad. (gran / grandes)

   ....

   (e) Mi abuela vive en el piso. (primera / primer)

   ....

Possessives and pronouns

1 Complete the table with the missing possessive adjectives.

English	Spanish singular	Spanish plural
my	mi	
your		tus
his / her / its		
our		nuestros / nuestras
your		
their	su	

2 Complete each sentence with the correct possessive adjective.

(a) My house is big. .... casa es grande.

(b) His brother is the oldest. .... hermano es el mayor.

(c) Their sons play tennis. .... hijos juegan al tenis.

(d) My favourite films are science fiction. .... películas preferidas son las de ciencia ficción.

(e) Its food is healthy. .... comida es sana.

> Possessive pronouns are like possessive adjectives but replace the noun they describe.
> They must agree with the noun they replace!
> In Spanish they are always accompanied by the definite article:
>
> | el mío / la mía / los míos / las mías = mine | el tuyo / la tuya = yours |
> |---|---|
> | el suyo / la suya = his / hers | el nuestro / la nuestra = ours |

3 Complete these comparisons with the correct possessive pronoun.

Example: Nuestras fotos no son tan buenas como las tuyas. (yours)
(Our photos are not as good as yours.)

(a) Tu perro es más listo que .... (mine)

(b) Mis gafas son menos grandes que .... (his)

(c) Tu profesor de historia es más estricto que .... (ours)

(d) Su uniforme es más cómodo que .... (yours)

4 Rewrite the phrases to create one sentence using the relative pronoun *que*.

Example: Tengo un hermano. Se llama Diego. → Tengo un hermano que se llama Diego.

(a) María tiene un gato. Es negro y pequeño.

....

(b) Vivimos en un pueblo. Está en el norte de Ecuador.

....

(c) En la clase de inglés tengo que leer un libro. Es muy aburrido.

....

Had a go ☐ Nearly there ☐ Nailed it! ☐   **Grammar**

Comparisons

> To form the comparative: **más** + adjective + **que** = more … than
> **menos** + adjective + **que** = less … than
> **tan** + adjective + **como** = as … as

1 Read the English and then complete each Spanish sentence with the correct comparative adjective.

   Example: My sister is taller than my brother.
   Mi hermana es *más alta que* mi hermano.

   (a) My mother is taller than my father.
       Mi madre es .... mi padre.

   (b) Luisa is less serious than Marcos.
       Luisa es .... Marcos.

   (c) This bus is slower than the train.
       Este autobús es .... el tren.

   (d) Fruit is as healthy as vegetables.
       La fruta es .... las verduras.

   (e) This shirt is as expensive as that jacket.
       Esta camisa es .... aquella chaqueta.

2 Write out the correct superlative sentence.

   > Remember!
   > *el / la mejor, los / las mejores* = the best
   > *el / la peor, los / las peores* = the worst

   Example: Esta falda es *la menos cara*. (the least expensive)

   (a) Mi profesor de inglés es .... (the best)

   (b) Mis deberes de religión son .... (the worst)

   (c) Mi mejor amiga es .... de la clase. (the smallest)

   (d) Estas novelas son .... (the most difficult)

   (e) Las películas de acción son .... (the least boring)

3 Translate these sentences **into Spanish**.

   > To translate words like 'incredibly' or 'extremely' don't forget to use the ending *-ísimo/a*.

   Example: My car is the cheapest. *Mi coche es el más barato.*

   (a) My cousin is stronger than your uncle. ....

   (b) Her mobile phone is incredibly small. ....

   (c) The Spanish exam is extremely easy. ....

   (d) Adventure films are as exciting as action films. ....

   (e) My school is the oldest. ....

   (f) Science is less boring than Maths. ....

   (g) My friend Omar is our best player. ....

97

Grammar

Had a go ☐ Nearly there ☐ Nailed it! ☐

Other adjectives

> Demonstrative adjectives are used to indicate which thing / person you are referring to ('this', 'those', etc). There are three in Spanish: one for 'this / these' and one for 'that / those'. Another version, meaning 'that / those over there', is needed at Higher tier only. All forms agree with their noun in number and gender.

1 Complete the table with the correct demonstrative adjective.

English	Masculine singular	Feminine singular	Masculine plural	Feminine plural
this / these	este			
that / those		esa		
that (over there) / those (over there)			aquellos	

2 Translate **into Spanish**. (o/t = 'over there')

(a) these jackets ....
(b) this T-shirt ....
(c) that girl (o/t) ....
(d) those eggs ....
(e) that mobile phone ....
(f) those magazines (o/t) ....
(g) this book ....
(h) that film ....
(i) that train (o/t) ....
(j) these hats ....
(k) those oranges ....
(l) those boys (o/t) ....

3 Complete the sentences with the correct indefinite adjectives from the box below.

> cada   todo / toda   algún / alguna   otro / otra
> mismo / misma   todos / todas   algunos / algunas
> otros / otras   mismos / mismas

(a) Juega al baloncesto .... (*every*) día.
(b) Siempre da la .... (*same*) opinión.
(c) Tengo .... (*some*) amigas que viven en Barcelona.
(d) Ayer, ... (*all*) los alumnos hicieron sus exámenes.
(e) Voy a hablar con Hugo porque él tiene .... (*another*) llave.

4 Fill in the gaps in the text using both demonstrative and indefinite adjectives. The text is translated for you below.

> El año pasado fui de vacaciones con mi familia. (a) .... los años vamos al sur de Inglaterra, pero este año fuimos a España. (b) .... de mis amigos han ido a España, pero esta fue mi primera vez. ¡Me gustó mucho! (c) .... los españoles que conocimos eran muy simpáticos y (d) .... hablaban muy bien inglés. En España, a los jóvenes les gusta la (e) .... ropa que a los jóvenes ingleses y nos divierten los (f) .... pasatiempos. ¡Fue muy interesante!

> Last year I went on holiday with my family. Every year we go to the south of England but this year we went to Spain. Some of my friends have been to Spain but this was my first time. I liked it a lot! All the Spanish people we met were really nice and some spoke very good English. In Spain, the young people love the same clothes as English young people and we like the same hobbies. It was really interesting!

Had a go ☐   Nearly there ☐   Nailed it! ☐

Grammar

Pronouns

1 Complete the tables with the correct subject pronouns **in English** or **Spanish**.

yo	
	you singular
	he
ella	

	we (masc.)
nosotras	
vosotros	
	you plural (fem.)
ellos	
	they (fem.)

> A pronoun replaces a noun. An object pronoun has the action (shown by the verb) done to it. It can be direct or indirect.
>
> She sent it to me. **it** = direct object; **me** = indirect object
>
> Direct object pronouns: *me*, *te*, *lo / la*, *nos*, *os*, *los / las*
>
> Position of the object pronouns:
>
> - Before a conjugated verb: *lo compro* (I buy it), *lo he comprado* (I have bought it)
> - After a negative: *no lo compro* (I don't buy it)
> - At the end of an infinitive or gerund (or before the verb): *voy a comprarlo / lo voy a comprar* (I am going to buy it), *estoy comprándolo / lo estoy comprando* (I am buying it)

2 Replace the noun with the correct object pronoun.

Example: Miguel ha perdido la carta. → *Miguel la ha perdido.*

(a) Hemos perdido las llaves. ....

(b) Han perdido la foto. ....

(c) Carmen come el bocadillo. ....

(d) Compro el vestido. ....

(e) No bebo leche. ....

(f) No lavo la ropa. ....

(g) Quiero escribir un correo electrónico. ....

(h) No quiero leer esa novela. ....

(i) Necesito la información ahora. ....

(j) Vamos a vender la casa. ....

> Remember!
> You only need to replace the noun. The verb will stay the same.

3 Translate these sentences, which use direct and indirect object pronouns, **into English** or **Spanish**.

Example: Le di mi cuaderno de matemáticas. → *I gave him my Maths exercise book.*

(a) Le voy a escribir esta tarde. ....

(b) Los visité ayer. ....

(c) Lo haré si tengo tiempo. ....

> Indirect object pronouns: *me*, *te*, *le*, *nos*, *os*, *les*

(d) Le di un regalo para su cumpleaños. ....

(e) ¿Las has visto? ....

(f) She came to visit me at home. ....

(g) They sent me the information. ....

(h) I am going to buy them (masc.) online. ....

Grammar

Had a go ☐ Nearly there ☐ Nailed it! ☐

The present tense

> To form the present tense, replace the infinitive ending with:
>
> *-ar* verbs: *o, as, a, amos, áis, an*
>
> *-er* verbs: *o, es, e, emos, éis, en*
>
> *-ir* verbs: *o, es, e, imos, ís, en*
>
> *Tú* is used for people you know and in the present tense the verb will always end in *s*.
>
> *Usted* is the formal word for 'you' and the verb takes the same ending as *él* or *ella*, and therefore has no *s* at the end.

1 Write the verb in the correct person.

Example: escuchar (tú) → *escuchas*

(a) vivir (nosotros) → ....

(b) bailar (ellas) → ....

(c) vender (yo) → ....

(d) llevar (vosotros) → ....

(e) odiar (tú) → ....

(f) comer (él) → ....

(g) salir (nosotros) → ....

(h) escuchar (usted) → ....

2 Choose the correct verb for each sentence.

Example: En mi tiempo libre (*practico*) / *practican* deportes.

(a) Mis padres *comemos* / *comen* mucha carne.

(b) Mi hermana y yo *vive* / *vivimos* en un barrio bonito.

(c) ¿A qué hora *tienes* / *tienen* tu clase de natación?

(d) Solo *habla* / *hablan* en francés cuando están solos.

(e) Usted *debes* / *debe* escribir aquí.

(f) Nuestro profesor es simpático y nunca *grita* / *gritáis*.

(g) Normalmente *chateas* / *chateo* con mis amigos por Internet.

(h) A veces su profesor *lee* / *leen* en clase.

(i) ¿Usted qué *piensa* / *pensáis* del precio de la ropa?

(j) *Puedes* / *Podéis* comprar vuestros billetes aquí.

> In the present tense, *-er* and *-ir* verbs only different for the *nosotros* and *vosotros* parts of the verb and so there are fewer endings to learn!

3 Write the correct part of the verb in each sentence. Watch out for radical-changing verbs!

Example: Mis amigos *estudian* inglés y español. (estudiar)

(a) Nos gusta la comida española y esta noche .... tapas. (cenar)

(b) Los artistas a veces .... al aire libre. (trabajar)

(c) Me levanto temprano y .... el desayuno a las ocho y media. (tomar)

(d) Limpia su dormitorio y luego .... la mesa. (poner)

(e) Nunca comemos chocolate, pero .... pasteles a menudo. (comprar)

(f) ¿Cuánto .... las verduras? (costar)

(g) .... un teléfono móvil, pero no tengo dinero. (querer)

(h) Los niños .... mucho hoy en día. (pedir)

Had a go ☐ Nearly there ☐ Nailed it! ☐

Grammar

Reflexive verbs

1. Write the correct reflexive pronouns next to each part of the verbs *levantarse* and *divertirse*.

	levanto
te	levantas
	levanta
	levantamos
	levantáis
se	levantan

	divierto
	diviertes
	divierte
	divertimos
	divertís
	divierten

2. Complete the sentence with the correct reflexive pronoun.

   Example: A veces mis amigos no *se* visten bien.

   (a) Normalmente, los sábados, ... levanta a las nueve y media.

   (b) Mis hermanos no .... llevan bien, pero yo me llevo bien con ellos.

   (c) ¿A qué hora .... despiertas los domingos?

   (d) Los profesores .... quejan mucho de sus alumnos.

   (e) Mis primos .... llaman Juan y Lola.

   (f) .... levantamos temprano para ir de vacaciones.

   (g) ¿Qué día .... casáis?

   (h) .... lavas y te vistes antes de ir al colegio.

3. Rewrite the story for Sofía. Change all the verbs in the 'I' form to the 'she' form. Don't forget to change the non-reflexive verbs too!

   > Todos los días me levanto temprano para ir a trabajar. Trabajo en una tienda de ropa famosa. Primero me lavo los dientes y luego me baño y me visto. Bajo las escaleras y tomo el desayuno. Siempre me siento en la cocina para comer. Después, me lavo la cara en el cuarto de baño que está abajo, al lado de la cocina. Me pongo la chaqueta y salgo a las ocho y media porque el autobús llega a las nueve menos cuarto. Vuelvo a casa a las siete de la tarde.

   Todos los días Sofía se levanta ....

   ....

   ....

   ....

   ....

   ....

   ....

   ....

   ....

   ....

   > Remember! Some verbs are regular but have an irregular ending in the first person singular. *Poner* is one of those verbs: *pongo, pones, pone,* etc. It can be reflexive when it means 'putting on' clothes. Watch out for *salir*, too – the first person singular is *salgo*.

Irregular verbs (present)

1 Choose the correct verb for each answer.

Example: Mis padres *decimos* / *dicen* que hablo demasiado.

(a) Yo no *tiene* / *tengo* la llave. ¿La *tienes* / *tenéis* tú?

(b) Paula le *dan* / *da* flores a nuestra madre y yo le *damos* / *doy* chocolates.

(c) Cuando mi padre *oigo* / *oye* mi música, *salgo* / *sale* de la habitación rápidamente.

(d) Si *haces* / *hace* buen tiempo, yo no *coge* / *cojo* el autobús.

(e) Alba, cuando tú y Marcos *vienes* / *venís* a casa, siempre *traen* / *traéis* regalos.

2 Complete the sentences with the correct form of the verb.

Example: A las ocho yo *salgo* (salir) de casa.

(a) Sube el volumen, Diego no .... (oír) muy bien.

(b) Nunca voy a Argentina y, por eso, no .... (conocer) Buenos Aires.

(c) Nuestros primos .... (venir) a cenar esta noche.

(d) Cuando voy a la ciudad siempre .... (coger) el tren.

(e) Cada año, mi familia y yo .... (ir) de vacaciones a España.

(f) Mis amigos han decidido sus asignaturas pero yo no .... (saber) qué hacer.

(g) Marta, ¿................................ (tener) tu móvil en tu bolsillo?

(h) Si hace frío en casa, simplemente me .... (poner) un jersey.

(i) Es el cumpleaños de Elena así que yo .... (traer) un pastel.

(j) Mis profesores .... (decir) que voy a sacar buenas notas.

3 Translate these sentences **into Spanish**.

(a) I go to Spain. ....

(b) He has two sisters. ....

(c) I hear music. ....

(d) She tells the truth. ....

(e) We catch the bus. ....

(f) They do their homework. ....

(g) You (*tú*) go out on Saturdays. ....

(h) I give classes. ....

(i) He brings bread. ....

(j) I put the fruit on the table. ....

Had a go ☐   Nearly there ☐   Nailed it! ☐

Grammar

Ser and estar

> **ser:** use for permanent things (e.g. nationality, occupation, colour, size, personality)
> **estar:** use for temporary things (e.g. illness, appearance, feelings) and location

1 Write the correct form of the verb *ser* or *estar*.

Example: *Somos* ingleses y vivimos en el norte del país. (ser – nosotros)

(a) ¿Dónde .... el banco? (estar)

(b) Mis abuelas .... muy simpáticas. (ser)

(c) .... de Madrid, pero trabajo en Barcelona. (ser – yo)

(d) El vestido .... verde con flores blancas. (ser)

(e) .... las cuatro y media de la tarde. (ser)

(f) El armario .... al lado de la puerta. (estar)

(g) .... muy tristes hoy porque las vacaciones han terminado. (estar – vosotros)

(h) .... listos para el examen de historia. (estar – nosotros)

2 Now translate the sentences from exercise 1 **into English**. In brackets, write down the reason why the verb is *ser* or *estar*.

Example: *We are English and we live in the north of the country.* (ser for nationalities)

(a) ....
(b) ....
(c) ....
(d) ....
(e) ....
(f) ....
(g) ....
(h) ....

3 Tick the phrases which use the correct verb 'to be'. Correct those which are wrong.

Example: Estoy en España de vacaciones. ✓

La plaza es a mano izquierda. ✗ La plaza está a mano izquierda.

(a) Somos españoles y hablamos castellano.

....

(b) Mi amigo está alto y tiene el pelo negro.

....

(c) Me duele la cabeza y soy enfermo.

....

(d) El árbol ha muerto y estoy muy triste.

....

(e) Su primo es cubano y trabaja como profesor.

....

(f) Mi madre está médica y mi padre está escritor.

....

103

The gerund / present participle

Had a go ☐   Nearly there ☐   Nailed it! ☐

> Gerunds are '-ing' words (playing, singing, etc.). To form them, replace the infinitive endings as follows:
> hablar → hablando, comer → comiendo, vivir → viviendo.
> Remember! Some verbs have irregular gerunds:
> caer → cayendo   oír → oyendo   leer → leyendo
> Some radical-changing -ir verbs also change their stem in the gerund:
> pedir → pidiendo   vestir → vistiendo

1 Change the following infinitives into the gerund, and write their meanings **in English**.

Example: beber → bebiendo – drinking

(a) comer → ....   (f) recibir → ....
(b) estudiar → ....   (g) escribir → ....
(c) correr → ....   (h) escuchar → ....
(d) tomar → ....   (i) aprender → ....
(e) decir → ....   (j) ver → ....

2 What are these people doing? Write sentences using the words from the box.

comer paella	correr en la calle	bailar flamenco
hablar con amigos	escuchar música	ver una película
navegar por Internet	escribir una carta	~~montar en bicicleta~~

Example: (she) Está montando en bicicleta.

(a) (I) ....   (c) (we) ....
(b) (they) ....   (d) (you singular) ....

3 Translate the first part of the sentences **into Spanish**.

> The imperfect continuous is formed using the imperfect tense of **estar** + the gerund:
> estaba comiendo – I was eating
> estar in the imperfect tense: estaba, estabas, estaba, estábamos, estabais, estaban

Example: (I was walking) Estaba paseando cuando me caí al agua.

(a) (she was playing basketball) .... cuando se rompió el dedo.
(b) (they were eating) .... cuando su madre les llamó.
(c) (we were sunbathing) .... cuando empezó a llover.
(d) (you were singing) .... cuando salió el tren.
(e) (we were watching TV) .... cuando nuestro hermanastro volvió a casa.
(f) (I was playing tennis) .... cuando llamó.
(g) (you all were listening to the teacher) .... cuando entró la directora.
(h) (he was studying in the library) .... cuando oyó el ruido.

Had a go ☐ Nearly there ☐ Nailed it! ☐

Grammar

The preterite tense

> The preterite tense is used to describe completed actions in the past. Replace the infinitive ending with:
>
> **-ar** verbs: *é, aste, ó, amos, asteis, aron*
>
> **-er** and **-ir** verbs: *í, iste, ió, imos, isteis, ieron*
>
> Remember! There are lots of irregular verbs in the preterite.
>
> At Foundation tier, you need to learn the irregular preterite tense of the verbs: *ser, ir, hacer, dar, decir, estar, poder, poner, querer, tener, traer* and *venir*.
>
> At Higher tier, you also need to know those verbs that have irregular spellings in the third person singular and plural, such as *pidió / pidieron, sintió / sintieron, leyó / leyeron*.
>
> At Higher tier, you should also be aware of the first person singular changes in *-car, -zar* and *-gar* verbs (e.g. *saqué, empecé* and *llegué*).

1 Write the verb in the correct form of the preterite tense.

   Example: comer (tú) → *comiste*

   (a) sacar (ellos) → ....
   (b) volver (nosotros) → ....
   (c) comprar (él) → ....
   (d) llegar (tú) → ....
   (e) trabajar (vosotros) → ....
   (f) ir (usted) → ....
   (g) dar (yo) → ....
   (h) tener (nosotros) → ....
   (i) pedir (ellas) → ....
   (j) leer (él) → ....

2 Complete the sentences with the verb in the correct form of the preterite. All these sentences use irregular verbs.

   (a) La semana pasada .... (ir) a casa de mis amigos.
   (b) Mi novio y yo no .... (tener) tiempo para visitar el museo.
   (c) Sus padres nos .... (dar) unos regalos bonitos.
   (d) Carmen .... (ir) a la playa con su hermano.
   (e) El chico me .... (dar) un café y yo .... (pagar) en seguida.
   (f) El invierno pasado mis padres .... (ir) de vacaciones solos.
   (g) 'No es verdad', ... (decir) el niño.
   (h) El concierto .... (ser) excelente. Me gustó mucho.
   (i) .... (hacer) mis deberes antes de jugar al fútbol.
   (j) Ayer .... (tener) que lavar el coche y luego salí con mis amigos.

3 Read the text in the present tense and rewrite the text, changing all the verbs in bold into the preterite.

   Voy al cine con mis amigos y **vemos** una película de acción. Después **comemos** en un restaurante. **Como** una hamburguesa con jamón y queso, y mi amiga Lola **come** pescado con patatas. **Bebemos** agua y mi amigo Tom **come** un pastel de chocolate, pero yo no **como** postre. Después del restaurante **voy** en tren a casa de mi prima. El viaje **es** largo y aburrido. **Vuelvo** a casa y **me acuesto** a las once de la noche.

   Fui al cine con mis amigos ....
   ....
   ....
   ....

Grammar

Had a go ☐ Nearly there ☐ Nailed it! ☐

The imperfect tense

> Remember! The imperfect is used:
> - to describe repeated actions in the past
> - when you would say 'used to' in English
> - to describe background details.
>
> Replace the infinitive ending with:
>
> **-ar** verbs: *aba, abas, aba, ábamos, abais, aban*
>
> **-er** and **-ir** verbs: *ía, ías, ía, íamos, íais, ían*
>
> At Foundation tier, you only need to know the first three (singular) forms of the verb in the imperfect tense.

1. Tick the sentences which contain imperfect verbs and underline the verbs.

   Example: Antes mi colegio <u>era</u> más pequeño. ✓

   (a) El miércoles fuimos al parque y jugamos al tenis durante una hora y media.

   (b) De pequeños, íbamos a la costa todos los veranos.

   (c) Había mucha gente en el museo y los cuadros eran muy bonitos.

   (d) Mi padre nos preparó una cena vegetariana.

   (e) Cuando eran más jóvenes, no comían ni fruta ni verdura.

   (f) Gabriela llegó a Madrid en tren para empezar su nuevo trabajo.

   (g) Ayer nos encontramos en el café y hablamos toda la tarde.

   (h) Estaba nervioso cada vez que hacía una prueba de matemáticas.

   (i) Lo pasé muy bien porque hizo sol y no llovió.

   (j) Nevaba todos los días y hacía un frío terrible.

2. Translate the sentences from exercise 1 **into English**. Explain your choice of tense in brackets. Write your answers on a separate piece of paper.

   Example: My school used to be smaller. (imperfect for 'used to')

3. Complete the sentences with the correct verb in the past tense. It could be either the preterite or the imperfect.

   Example: El sábado <u>fuimos</u> a la discoteca a bailar y a divertirnos. (ir)

   (a) Cuando mi hermana .... tres años empezó a tocar el piano. (tener)

   (b) Mi familia .... en el campo, pero ahora tiene un piso en Barcelona. (vivir)

   (c) .... lloviendo cuando llegamos al camping. (estar)

   (d) La semana pasada .... el coche y limpié la cocina. (lavar)

   (e) Todos los días .... en el jardín y cuidaban las flores. (trabajar)

   (f) Hizo compras por Internet y .... mucho dinero. (gastar)

   (g) Siempre .... fruta y bebíamos mucha agua para estar en forma. (comer)

   (h) Una vez .... al tenis con mi profesor de inglés, pero no gané. (jugar)

Had a go ☐ **Nearly there** ☐ **Nailed it!** ☐

Grammar

The future tense

> The **immediate future** tense is used to say what's going to happen. It is formed using the present tense of *ir* + *a* + an infinitive: *Voy a salir a las dos*. (I'm going to go out at two o'clock.)
> Present tense of *ir*: *voy, vas, va, vamos, vais, van*
> At Foundation tier, you only need to know the first three (singular) forms of the verb in the future tense.

1. Complete the sentences with the missing parts of the immediate future tense.

    Example: I am going to buy a dress. → Voy a comprar un vestido.

    (a) We are going to play basketball. Vamos a .... al baloncesto.

    (b) He is going to sunbathe. .... a tomar el sol.

    (c) They are going to eat fish and chips. Van .... comer pescado y patatas fritas.

    (d) I am not going to cry. No .... a llorar.

    (e) Are you going to watch the film? ¿............... a ver la película?

    (f) You (all) are going to listen and repeat. .... a escuchar y a repetir.

    (g) My mother is going to catch the bus. Mi madre .... a coger el autobús.

    (h) My friends are going to go to the UK. Mis amigos van a .... al Reino Unido.

    (i) We are not going to work on Saturdays. No .... a trabajar los sábados.

    (j) I am going to go out with my girlfriend. .... a salir con mi novia.

2. Write the Spanish for these sentences. Remember to use the future tense when describing what will happen.

    > The **future tense** is used to talk about what you will do or what will happen in the future. The future tense is formed by adding these endings onto the infinitive:
    > *-é, -ás, -á, -emos, -éis, -án*
    > Don't forget the accents!
    > Remember there are some irregular future verbs: *saldré, diré, tendré, haré, podré, pondré, querré, sabré, vendré*.

    Example: I will buy a dress. *Compraré un vestido.*

    (a) We are going to watch the film. ....

    (b) I will not work on Mondays. ....

    (c) They are going to catch the underground. ....

    (d) He will go to the United Kingdom. ....

    (e) They are going to play with my brother. ....

    (f) You will go to Spain. ....

3. Complete the text with the correct verbs in the immediate future tense.

    | pasar | ser | ir | visitar | ir | viajar | probar | vivir |

    El año próximo mi amiga (a) .... a la universidad a estudiar matemáticas. Yo no (b) .... a la universidad porque (c) .... seis meses trabajando para ganar experiencia. Durante este tiempo (d) .... con mis padres para ahorrar dinero. Después, (e) .... por Europa con mi amiga, Elena. Juntas, (f) .... todos los sitios de interés y (g) .... toda la comida tradicional de cada país. (h) .... muy divertido!

Grammar

Had a go ☐ Nearly there ☐ Nailed it! ☐

The conditional tense

> The conditional is used to describe what you would do or what would happen in the future. To form the conditional, add the following endings to the infinitive:
>
> ía, ías, ía, íamos, íais, ían
>
> There are a few verbs with irregular stems and these are the same as those in the future tense.
>
> At Foundation tier, you only need to know the first three (singular) forms of the verb in the conditional tense.

1 Change these future tense verbs into the conditional. Write the English for each.

   Example: haré → haría – I would do

   (a) compraremos → ....
   (b) saldrán → ....
   (c) trabajaréis → ....
   (d) estará → ....
   (e) jugarás → ....
   (f) vendremos → ....
   (g) podrás → ....
   (h) habrá → ....

2 In an ideal world, what would happen next year? Create conditional sentences using words from the box.

   Example: Mi madre compraría un perro.

   (a) Mi profesor .... de vacaciones.
   (b) Nuestros primos .... el sol en la playa.
   (c) El jefe no .... todos los días.
   (d) Mis amigos y yo .... mucho dinero.
   (e) No .... polución del aire.
   (f) Más gente .... el transporte público.
   (g) Nadie .... hambre.
   (h) Los gobiernos .... contra el cambio climático.
   (i) Mi equipo de fútbol .... la competición nacional.
   (j) Mi hermano y yo no .... el dormitorio.

   ```
   tener
   ir
   ganar
   haber
   compartir
   comprar
   trabajar
   usar
   luchar
   tomar
   ganar
   ```

3 Give advice using the conditional of *deber* or *poder* to help these people.

   Example: Tengo dolor de cabeza.
              Deberías / Podrías dormirte un poco.

   (a) No puedo dormir.
   ....

   (b) Como demasiado chocolate.
   ....

   (c) No tengo energía.
   ....

   (d) Estoy enfermo.
   ....

   (e) Estoy cansado todo el tiempo.
   ....

   (f) Me duelen los dientes.
   ....

   ```
   dormirte un poco
   acostarte temprano
   comer más frutas y verdura
   ir al médico
   ir al dentista
   hacer más ejercicio
   leer para relajarte
   ```

Had a go ☐ Nearly there ☐ Nailed it! ☐

Grammar

The perfect tense

> The perfect tense is used to talk about what someone **has done** or what **has happened**.
> It is formed by taking the present tense of *haber* + a past participle.
>
> To form the past participle, replace the infinitive ending with:
>
> -*ar* verbs: -*ado*
>
> -*er* and -*ir* verbs: -*ido*

1 Complete the table with the correct parts of the verb *haber* and the past participle endings.

	haber (in present tense) (I have ..., etc.)	+ past participle (spoken, eaten, lived, etc.)
yo	he	
tú		habl...
él / ella / usted		com...
nosotros / nosotras	hemos	viv...
vosotros / vosotras		
ellos / ellas / ustedes		

2 Unscramble the anagrams of irregular past participles in the third column and write the correct version in the second column next to its infinitive.

Infinitive	Irregular past participle	Scrambled version
hacer		beatiro
volver		cheoh
abrir		cidoh
romper		lutove
ver		sotupe
escribir		tisvo
poner		toro
decir		triseco

3 Translate sentences (a) to (e) **into English** and (f) to (j) **into Spanish**.

Example: He hablado con él. I have spoken to him.

(a) Hemos perdido el coche. ....

(b) ¿Has estudiado español? ....

(c) Han comprado un portátil. ....

(d) He hecho mis deberes. ....

(e) Hemos visto un programa muy informativo. ....

(f) I have broken my arm. ....

(g) They have lost their keys. ....

(h) We have drunk lots of tea. ....

(i) Have you visited the museum today? ....

(j) The teachers have opened the windows. ....

Grammar

Had a go ☐ Nearly there ☐ Nailed it! ☐

Giving instructions

> To give commands:
> – to one person (**tú**): use the 'you' singular form of the present tense, minus the final **s**:
> ¡*Escucha!* Listen! ¡*Abre!* Open!
> – to more than one person (**vosotros**): change the final **r** of the infinitive to **d**:
> ¡*Escuchad!* Listen! ¡*Abrid!* Open!
> Irregular *tú* commands include:
>
> | | decir | hacer | ir | ser | poner | salir | tener | venir |
> |---------|-------|-----------|----|-----|-------|-------|-------|-------|
> | tú | di | haz | ve | sé | pon | sal | ten | ven |
> | English | say | make / do | go | be | put | leave | have | come |

1 Change the following infinitives into familiar singular commands (*tú*). Be careful – some are irregular in command form.

Example: Hablar más ⟶ Habla más.

(a) Subir a la derecha ⟶ .... (f) Cantar más bajo ⟶ ....

(b) Cruzar la plaza ⟶ .... (g) Leer en voz alta ⟶ ....

(c) Decir tu nombre ⟶ .... (h) Escuchar bien ⟶ ....

(d) Tener cuidado ⟶ .... (i) Beber el agua ⟶ ....

(e) Venir aquí ⟶ .... (j) Hacer este ejercicio ⟶ ....

2 Now change the above commands into familiar plural ones (*vosotros*). Remember, to form the *vosotros* commands, you change the *r* of the infinitive to *d*.

Example: Habla más. ⟶ Hablad más.

(a) .... (f) ....

(b) .... (g) ....

(c) .... (h) ....

(d) .... (i) ....

(e) .... (j) ....

3 Translate these sentences **into Spanish**.

tú commands	*vosotros/las* commands
(a) Download the music.	(a) Buy the vegetables in the market.
(b) Make the bed.	(b) Choose your bedrooms.
(c) Visit the museum.	(c) Discuss the problem first.
(d) Sing with the music.	(d) Recycle those bottles.

Had a go ☐   Nearly there ☐   Nailed it! ☐

Grammar

 # The present subjunctive

> The subjunctive is used in a range of contexts, such as:
> - after *cuando* when the action of the verb has not yet taken place: *Cuando sea mayor, voy a viajar a Bolivia.* When I am older, I'm going to travel to Bolivia.
> - after *para que* (so that …): *Te mandaré la carta hoy para que la tengas antes de lunes.* I'll send you the letter today so that you have it before Monday.
> - after verbs of wishing, commanding or requesting + *que*: *Quiero que vayas a pedir ayuda.* I want you to go and ask for help.
> - after verbs of emotion + *que*: *Estoy muy contenta de que vengas a la fiesta.* I am very glad that you are coming to the party.
>
> These are the five verbs that you need to know in the singular forms:
> *hacer* (*haga, hagas*), *ser* (*sea, seas*), *venir* (*venga, vengas*), *tener* (*tenga, tengas*), *ir* (*vaya, vayas*)
> The third person singular is the same as the first person singular.

1 Change these verbs from the present tense to the present subjunctive:

(a) hace → ....   (f) tengo → ....
(b) tienes → ....   (g) soy → ....
(c) vengo → ....   (h) va → ....
(d) es → ....   (i) hago → ....
(e) vas → ....   (j) vienes → ....

2 Complete the sentences with the verb in the correct form of the present subjunctive.

Example: Cuando vayas a la cama, apaga la luz.

(a) Cuando .... a pasear, ponte un sombrero porque hace mucho sol. (ir)
(b) Te daré mi móvil para que .... una foto. (hacer)
(c) Me sorprende que .... inglesa; pensé que eras española. (ser)
(d) Mis abuelos prefieren que yo .... en marzo este año. (venir)
(e) Mi marido quiere que .... una fiesta para mi cumpleaños. (tener)
(f) Cuando .... diecinueve años te permitiré viajar por Europa en tren. (tener)
(g) Mi profesor me ha dicho que .... los deberes otra vez. (hacer)
(h) Me molesta que nuestro vecino .... un perro tan grande en ese piso pequeño. (tener)

3 Translate the sentences **into Spanish**.

(a) My sister wants me to make a cake.

....

(b) It annoys me that you do not come with me.

....

(c) I hope that you are lucky with the exams.

....

(d) When you go to Spain you must visit Barcelona.

....

(e) You can go to the Canary Islands when you are older.

....

Grammar

Had a go ☐   Nearly there ☐   Nailed it! ☐

Negatives

> To make a sentence negative, use **no** in front of the whole verb:
> *No me gusta la música clásica.*   I don't like classical music.
> *No vamos a visitar el palacio.*   We are not going to visit the palace.

1 Write these sentences in the negative.

   Example: Tengo clase hoy a las diez. → *No tengo clase hoy a las diez.*

   (a) Estudio geografía. → ....

   (b) Vamos a la ciudad. → ....

   (c) Ricardo compró una bicicleta nueva. → ....

   (d) Sus padres vieron la tele. → ....

   (e) Voy a ir a España la semana próxima. → ....

2 Match the English and Spanish phrases.

   1 no ... nada   A never
   2 no ... nadie   B no / not any
   3 nunca   C not ... either
   4 no ... ningún / ninguna   D not ... or
   5 ya no   E no one / nobody
   6 no ... tampoco   F neither ... nor
   7 no ... ni   G not ... any more
   8 ni ... ni   H nothing / not ... anything

3 Rewrite the sentences with the negative words.

   Example: Marta habla de sus problemas. (nunca) → *Marta nunca habla de sus problemas.*

   > Note that *ninguno* must agree with the noun it precedes: *ninguna palabra* (no word)

   (a) Mis profesores gritan si hago una pregunta. (nunca) ....

   (b) Como durante el descanso. (no, nada) ....

   (c) En mi familia tuvimos un perro. (nunca) ....

   (d) Aquí tengo vestidos, faldas y camisetas. (no, ni, ni, ni) ....

   (e) Vas a comprar un coche. (no, ningún) ....

   (f) Mis padres escuchan. (no, a nadie) ....

4 Translate the sentences **into Spanish**. Be careful with the word order.

   Example: He never plays football when it rains. → *Nunca juega al fútbol cuando llueve.*

   (a) In the afternoon we never drink coffee. ....

   (b) I don't sing, dance or play any musical instruments. ....

   (c) They do not speak any languages. ....

   (d) We can't talk to anybody during the exam. ....
   ....

   (e) I will never smoke because it is bad for your health. ....
   ....

112

Had a go ☐ Nearly there ☐ Nailed it! ☐

Grammar

Special verbs

> A few verbs like *gustar* are generally used in the third person with a pronoun:
> *Me gusta bailar.* I like dancing.
>
> If the thing that is liked is plural, you use *me gustan*: *Me gustan los perros.* I like dogs.
>
> *encantar, doler, interesar* and *faltar* (*faltar* = Higher only) behave in the same way:
> *Le duele la cabeza.* His head hurts.
> *Faltan dos páginas.* Two pages are missing.
> *¿Te interesa la historia?* Are you interested in history?

1 Complete the table with the correct pronouns.

		I like
me	*gusta* (sing.)	you like
	gustan (pl.)	he / she / it likes

		we like
	gusta (sing.)	you (all) like
	gustan (pl.)	they like

> Remember! If the impersonal verb is followed by an infinitive, the singular form is used:
> *Le gusta cocinar.* He likes cooking.
>
> When the subject is a noun or a proper noun, you need to use *a*:
> *A Luisa le gusta salir a correr.* Luisa likes going for a run.

2 Complete the sentences.

Example: No ……………………… abrir la ventana. (*importar, I*)
No me importa abrir la ventana.

(a) ……………………………………… ir al mercado los martes. (*gustar, Paula*)

(b) ¿……………………………………… las tapas en este restaurante? (*gustar, you singular*)

(c) ……………………………………… visitar el castillo algún día. (*interesar, we*)

(d) ……………………………………… la cabeza. (*doler, Manuel*)

(e) ……………………………………… jugar a juegos con la videoconsola. (*encantar, he*)

(f) No ……………………………………… el calor. (*importar, I*)

[H only]
(g) ……………………………………… practicar más. (*hacer falta, I*)

(h) ……………………………………… arroz para hacer la paella. (*faltar, she*)

> Remember!
> *acabar* (in the present tense) + *de* + infinitive ⟶ to have just …
> *llevar* (in the present tense) + time + gerund / present participle ⟶ has / have been … ing for + time
> **[H only]**

[H only] 3 Translate the sentences **into Spanish**.

(a) I have just seen a really good film. ………………………………………………………

(b) She has been working in the garden for two hours. …………………………………

(c) Nadim has just finished his university course. ………………………………………

(d) We have been living here for a month. ………………………………………………

(e) Your grandparents have just gone out. ………………………………………………

(f) I have been studying Spanish for three years. ………………………………………

Grammar

Had a go ☐ Nearly there ☐ Nailed it! ☐

Por and *para*

> Remember that *por* and *para* don't just mean 'for'. They can be translated in various ways depending on the sentence. For example: in, in order to, per, instead of.

1 Translate these sentences, which use *para*, **into English**.

(a) Para mi cumpleaños quiero un móvil nuevo.

....

(b) Mi amiga trabaja para una empresa internacional.

....

(c) Las aplicaciones para iPhone son increíbles.

....

(d) Como muchas verduras y pescado para estar en forma.

....

(e) Necesitas la llave para entrar en casa.

....

(f) Fumar es muy malo para la salud.

....

2 Rewrite the sentences with the word *por* in the correct place.

Example: Muchas gracias los pantalones. Muchas gracias por los pantalones.

(a) El coche rojo pasó las calles antiguas.

....

(b) Normalmente la mañana me gusta tomar huevos con pan.

....

(c) Mandé la información correo electrónico.

....

(d) Me gustaría cambiar este jersey otro.

....

(e) En la tienda ganamos quince euros a la hora.

....

3 Complete the sentences with either *por* or *para*.

Example: Por la tarde prefiero descansar.

(a) .... mantener la salud, lo más importante es beber mucha agua.

(b) Mis amigas compraron unas flores .... la profesora.

(c) Tengo que cambiar este libro .... otro.

(d) Los alumnos tienen que terminar los ejercicios .... el lunes.

Had a go ☐   Nearly there ☐   Nailed it! ☐

Grammar

Asking questions

> Don't forget that Spanish question words have accents. They also have an inverted question mark (¿) at the beginning, as well as a normal one at the end.

1. Use the question words in the box to complete the table below.

   ¿Qué?   ¿Cuánto?   ¿Dónde?   ¿Cuándo?   ¿Cuáles?
   ¿Adónde?   ¿Por qué?   ¿Cuántos?   ¿Cómo?   ¿Cuál?

Why?	
What?	¿Qué?
When?	
How?	
Where?	
Where to?	
Which?	¿Cuál?
Which ones?	
How much?	
How many?	

2. Complete the sentences with the correct question word.
   (a) ¿………………….. vive Mario?
   (b) ¿………………….. vais a llegar, chicos?
   (c) ¿………………….. de estas gafas son mías?
   (d) ¿………………….. dinero voy a necesitar para las vacaciones?
   (e) ¿………………….. piensas de la nueva profesora?
   (f) ¿………………….. vamos a viajar? ¿En metro o en autobús?
   (g) ¿………………….. vas a llevar a tus amigos cuando vengan?
   (h) ¿………………….. personas había en el estadio para el partido?

3. Match the correct answers to the questions.

1	¿Por qué te pones ese traje?
2	¿Qué compraste en el mercado?
3	¿Dónde encontraste mi móvil?
4	¿Cómo se comportó esta semana?
5	¿Cuándo tenemos el examen?
6	¿Cuáles quieres?
7	¿A cuántos kilómetros está?
8	¿Cuánto tiempo necesitas para terminar?

A	En la cocina, sobre la mesa.
B	Es el próximo lunes.
C	Esos, los más grandes, por favor.
D	Es que tengo una entrevista hoy.
E	Unos veinte. No está muy lejos.
F	No voy a tardar más de diez minutos.
G	Solo fruta y verduras.
H	Muy bien. Ningún problema.

Grammar

Had a go ☐ Nearly there ☐ Nailed it! ☐

The passive

> Remember that the passive can be formed in two ways. Firstly, like in English, you can use the verb *ser* (in the appropriate tense) followed by the past participle. Don't forget to make the past participle agree with the noun it refers to: **La cantante** *fue acompañada por la orquesta*. The singer was accompanied by the orchestra.

1 Complete the sentences with the correct form of the verb *ser* and the past participle. Be careful with the tense of *ser*.

(a) La novela .... el siglo pasado. (escribir)

(b) Los pisos .... el año próximo. (construir)

(c) El centro deportivo .... por miles de personas cada semana. (usar)

(d) Las instalaciones .... todos los días. (limpiar)

(e) Esta mañana los estudiantes .... a la directora. (presentar)

(f) Anoche la actriz .... varias veces en el restaurante. (reconocer)

(g) Normalmente los turistas .... en las islas. (aceptar)

(h) Debido a la nieve ayer, los niños .... a casa. (mandar)

2 Translate the sentences above **into English**.

(a) ....
(b) ....
(c) ....
(d) ....
(e) ....
(f) ....
(g) ....
(h) ....

> The other way to form the passive is to make the verb reflexive. The verb will usually be third person singular ('it') or third person plural ('they').
> *No se admiten perros.* Dogs (they) are not allowed. → plural verb needed.
> *Se sirve el desayuno entre las siete y las nueve.* Breakfast (it) is served between 7 and 9. → singular verb needed.

3 Complete the sentences with the correct tense in the reflexive form of the passive.

Future

(a) .... los resultados el lunes próximo. (publicar)

(b) .... las cartas a todos los estudiantes. (mandar)

Present

(c) La película .... en una novela clásica. (basar)

(d) .... una fiesta para los niños cada año. (organizar)

Preterite

(e) .... la habitación a las diez ayer. (limpiar)

(f) .... varios móviles y portátiles de la tienda. (robar)

Had a go ☐ Nearly there ☐ Nailed it! ☐

Grammar

Numbers

1 Write the numbers.

Example: trece 13

(a) veinte ....
(b) cuarenta y ocho ....
(c) nueve ....
(d) cien ....
(e) catorce ....
(f) mil ....
(g) trescientos ....
(h) cincuenta y siete ....
(i) veintitrés ....
(j) quince ....
(k) diecinueve ....
(l) quinientos ....
(m) un millón ....
(n) novecientos ....
(o) ochenta y ocho ....
(p) setenta y seis ....
(q) sesenta y siete ....
(r) diez ....
(s) cero ....
(t) veintinueve ....

> Ordinal numbers (*primero, segundo, tercero,* etc.) are not used for dates, except for *primero*, which can be used. Both of these are correct:
> *el uno de diciembre*
> *el primero de diciembre*

2 Write these dates and years **in Spanish**.

Example: 4 May *el cuatro de mayo*

(a) 1999 ....
(b) 10 October ....
(c) 1 January ....
(d) 3 March ....
(e) 2013 ....
(f) 16 November ....
(g) 30 May ....
(h) 1968 ....
(i) 2002 ....
(j) 21 April ....

> To give the time, use *son las* + the number for the hour, except for 'one o'clock', which is *Es la una*.
> *Son las ocho.* It's eight o'clock.
> For times **past** the hour, add *y cinco, y diez,* etc. *Son las nueve y veinte.* It is twenty past nine.
> For times **to** the hour, add *menos veinte, menos diez,* etc. *Son las tres menos diez.* It is ten to three.
>   a quarter past = *y cuarto*   a quarter to = *menos cuarto*   half past = *y media*

3 Write these times **in Spanish**.

Example: It's 5.25. *Son las cinco y veinticinco.*

(a) It's 7.15. ....
(b) It's 1.25. ....
(c) It's 8.35. ....
(d) It's 11.10. ....
(e) It's 3.45. ....
(f) It's 9.50. ....
(g) It's 5.30. ....
(h) It's 12.00. ....

Practice papers

Had a go ☐ Nearly there ☐ Nailed it! ☐

Paper 1: Speaking (Foundation)

Pearson Edexcel publishes official Sample Assessment Material on its website. This test has been written to help you practise what you have learned across the four skills and may not be representative of a real exam paper.

Track 103

Read aloud

My personal world

1 Marta, your friend, has written about her best friends. Read out the text below.

> Mis dos mejores amigas son muy diferentes.
> Ana es divertida y me hace reír.
> Es rubia con el pelo largo.
> María es más seria y muy tranquila.
> Tiene los ojos marrones y es bastante baja.

Now listen to the recording and answer two questions related to what you have read. You are expected to say a few words or a short phrase / sentence in response to each question. One-word answers will not be sufficient to gain full marks.

(12 marks)

Track 104

2 **Role play**

Setting: In the tourist office

Scenario: You are in the tourist office to ask for information on trips.

Listen to the recording of the teacher's part. The teacher will play the part of the tourist office employee and will speak first. They will ask questions **in Spanish** and you must answer **in Spanish**. You are expected to say a few words or a short phrase / sentence in response to each prompt. One-word answers will not be sufficient to gain full marks.

> **Task:**
> 1 Say where you want to go on the trip.
> 2 Say what day you would like to go.
> 3 Say how many people it is for.
> 4 Give your opinion about your holidays.
> 5 Ask a question about the time of the trip.

(10 marks)

Picture-based task

Picture 1
See this photo in colour

Picture 2
See this photo in colour

Track 105

3 Describe **ONE** of these pictures. Your description must cover:

- people
- location
- activity.

When you have finished your description, play the recording to hear and answer two questions relating to your chosen picture. You are expected to say a few words or a short phrase / sentence in response to each question. One-word answers will not be sufficient to gain full marks.

(12 marks)

Track 106

You will then move on to a conversation on the broader thematic context of **Studying and my future**. During the conversation, you will answer questions in the present, past and future tenses. Your responses should be as full and detailed as possible.

(16 marks)

TOTAL FOR PAPER = 50 MARKS

Had a go ☐ Nearly there ☐ Nailed it! ☐

Practice papers

Paper 2: Listening (Foundation)

Technology

Track 107

1 Luis, Julia and Antonio are talking about technology. What do they say? Listen to the recording and complete the sentences by putting a cross [×] in the correct box for each question.

(a) In the afternoons, Luis plays …

☐	A football.
☐	B on his games console.
☐	C in a band.

(b) Julia is buying a new …

☐	A mobile.
☐	B laptop.
☐	C app.

(c) Antonio thinks it is useful …

☐	A to text his friends.
☐	B to send emails.
☐	C to shop online.

(3 marks)

Hotel accommodation

Track 108

2 Manuel is talking about a hotel he stayed in. What aspects of the hotel does he mention? Listen to the recording and put a cross [×] in each one of the **three** correct boxes.

☐ A restaurant	☐ C swimming pool	☐ E games room
☐ B bedroom	☐ D gardens	☐ F views

(3 marks)

Transport

Track 109

3 Pilar is talking in a podcast. What does she say about transport in her area? Complete the gap in each sentence using a word from the box below. There are more words / phrases than gaps.

> car   train   bus   underground
> fun   easy   dangerous

(a) Pilar goes into town by ……………………………………………………………

(b) She gets around town by ……………………………………………………………

(c) She thinks cycling in town is ……………………………………………………………

(3 marks)

School

Track 110

4 Daniel is talking to his mother about getting a new uniform. What does he say he needs? Listen to the recording and put a cross [×] in each one of the **three** correct boxes.

☐ A trousers	☐ C jacket	☐ E shirt
☐ B socks	☐ D shoes	☐ F tie

(3 marks)

TV and film

Track 111

5 Alba is talking about TV and film. What does she say? Listen to the recording and complete the sentences by putting a cross [×] in the correct box for each question.

(a) Alba thinks going to the cinema is …

☐	A boring.
☐	B expensive.
☐	C cool.

(b) Her favourite series is …

☐	A a cooking competition.
☐	B a painting programme.
☐	C a dance show.

119

Practice papers

Had a go ☐ Nearly there ☐ Nailed it! ☐

(c) She thinks the people that do best in the series are …

☐	A singers.
☐	B actors.
☐	C sportspeople.

(d) The winners are generally …

☐	A women.
☐	B older people.
☐	C young.

(4 marks)

At the doctor's

Track 112

6 Diego is talking to the doctor. What does the doctor tell him? Listen to the recording and complete the following tables **in English**. You do not need to write in full sentences.

(a) What caused Daniel's headache	
(b) What he must do this afternoon	
(c) What he must do for the next two days	

(3 marks)

Sports

Track 113

7 David is talking about his favourite football player. What does he say? Listen to the recording and complete the sentences by putting a cross [×] in the correct box for each question.

(a) The footballer currently plays …

☐	A for an African team.
☐	B in Spain.
☐	C for his country.

(b) The player …

☐	A trains hard with the team.
☐	B is well respected by the fans.
☐	C is fast and very fit.

(c) In the last match, he …

☐	A was injured.
☐	B scored the winning goal.
☐	C could not play as he was ill.

(3 marks)

Holidays

Track 114

8 Lola is talking about the town where she goes on holiday. What does she say? Complete the gap in each sentence using a word or phrase from the box below. There are more words / phrases than gaps.

> countryside   sea   old town   city centre
> rents a flat   owns a house   stays on a campsite
> on the beach   reading   sunbathing   in the pool

(a) Tourists go mainly to the ……………………………………………………………

(b) Some never go to the ……………………………………………………………

(c) In the town, Lola ……………………………………………………………

(d) The children spend their time ……………………………………………………………

(e) The adults spend their time ……………………………………………………………

(5 marks)

Eating out

Track 115

9 Miguel is talking about a meal in a restaurant. What does he mention?
Listen to the recording and put a cross [×] in each one of the **three** correct boxes.

☐ A starters	☐ D service
☐ B vegetarian options	☐ E desserts
☐ C drinks	☐ F cost

(3 marks)

120

Had a go ☐   Nearly there ☐   Nailed it! ☐

Practice papers

A healthy lifestyle

10 Ana, Iván and Karima are talking about their lifestyles. What do they say? Listen to the recording and complete the sentences by putting a cross [×] in the correct box for each question.

(a) Ana thinks she should …

☐ **A** try a team sport.
☐ **B** do more exercise.
☐ **C** get more sleep.

(b) She plans to …

☐ **A** do more walking.
☐ **B** eat more healthily.
☐ **C** get more fresh air.

(c) Iván needs to stop …

☐ **A** watching films too late.
☐ **B** going on the internet at bedtime.
☐ **C** reading when he should be asleep.

(d) Karima is going to …

☐ **A** go to study sessions.
☐ **B** attend a book club.
☐ **C** start a new hobby.

(4 marks)

Future opportunities

11 (a) Marcos is talking about the school Careers Day. What does he say? Listen to the recording and answer the following questions **in English**. You do not need to write in full sentences.

(i) What does Marcos want to find out today? .... **(1 mark)**

(ii) What do his teachers think he will achieve in the exams? .... **(1 mark)**

(b) Carla and Alejandro are talking about their studies. What do they like and dislike about them? Listen to the recording and complete the following tables **in English**. You do not need to write in full sentences.

(i) Carla

likes …	
dislikes …	

(ii) Alejandro

likes …	
dislikes …	

(4 marks)
(Total for Question 11 = 6 marks)

Dictation

12 You are going to hear someone talking about their family. Sentences 1–3: write down the missing words in the gaps provided. In each gap, you will write one word **in Spanish**.

Example: *Soy una persona agradable*.

1 Nuestra .... tiene dos ....

2 Mi .... no tiene mucha ....

3 Me .... bien con mis ....

Sentences 4–6: write down the full sentences that you hear in the spaces provided, **in Spanish**.

Example: *Vive en el centro.*

4 ....

5 ....

6 ....

(10 marks)

TOTAL FOR PAPER = 50 MARKS

Paper 3: Reading (Foundation)

Caring for the environment

1 Read these comments from an internet forum.

> **Toni:** Normalmente, me gusta ir al colegio en bicicleta. Mis amigos y yo limpiamos el bosque cerca de mi casa.
>
> **Sara:** Siempre voy a pie al instituto. Apago las luces en casa cuando no se necesitan.
>
> **Emilio:** Reciclo todas las bolsas de plástico en casa. Intento no usar mucha agua.

Who says what? Choose the correct answers. Put a cross [×] in the correct column for each question.

	Who …	Toni	Sara	Emilio
(a)	… turns off lights?			
(b)	… cycles to school?			
(c)	… recycles plastic bags?			
(d)	… is careful with water?			
(e)	… cleans the local woods?			
(f)	… walks to school?			

(6 marks)

A shopping trip

2 Read Sofía's text message.

> Hola
> Voy a la ciudad esta tarde para comprar ropa. Voy con el dinero que recibí para mi cumpleaños. Iré a la tienda de ropa al lado de la estación primero, porque las cosas allí no son demasiado caras. Creo que buscaré también en el mercado porque allí vi unas camisetas bonitas en el pasado.

Put a cross [×] in each one of the **three** correct boxes.

Sofía …

☐ A wants to buy clothes.		☐ D doesn't want anything too expensive.
☐ B is buying a birthday present.		☐ E says there is no market today.
☐ C will try the shop next to the bank.		☐ F is looking for a T-shirt.

(3 marks)

Sports activities

3 Read this programme of activities.

> Si los niños en tu familia están aburridos durante las vacaciones, aquí organizamos varias actividades para los meses de verano. Por las mañanas, hay clases de tenis y por las tardes, tenemos competiciones de vóleibol para los jóvenes, con un *regalo* para el equipo que gana.

Had a go ☐ Nearly there ☐ Nailed it! ☐ **Practice papers**

(a) Complete the sentences below. Put a cross [×] in the correct box for each question.

(i) The activities are for …

☐ **A** the whole family.
☐ **B** bored children.
☐ **C** talented players.

(ii) They are being held …

☐ **A** through the summer months.
☐ **B** every weekend.
☐ **C** for six weeks.

(b) Which of these is the best translation for the word *regalo*?

Put a cross [×] in the correct box.

☐ **A** gift
☐ **B** match
☐ **C** draw

(3 marks)

A visit to the cinema

4 Read Paula and Malek's comments in a blog. Complete the following tables **in English**. You do not need to write in full sentences.

Paula
He visto muchas películas de ese director y normalmente son buenas. Pero la última es muy lenta y difícil de comprender.
En la otra sala, hay una película que es una historia de amor. Voy a verla la semana próxima.

(a) Paula

One opinion of the director's last film	....	(1 mark)
What film is on the other screen	....	(1 mark)

Malek
Lo peor de ir al cine es el ruido que hacen las otras personas. Siempre están comiendo algo o hablando demasiado alto.
Prefiero estar en casa porque puedo parar la película cuando quiero.

(b) Malek

One reason the cinema is noisy	....	(1 mark)
Why he prefers to watch at home	....	(1 mark)

(Total for Question 4 = 4 marks)

Local events

5 Read this article from a local web page.

> El día cuatro de enero muchas de las carreteras en el centro de la ciudad estarán cerradas a los coches por la mañana. Están preparando las calles para la fiesta del día después y el evento religioso del viernes. Si tienes que ir a la ciudad, recomendamos dejar el coche en casa.
>
> Parece que no vamos a tener buen tiempo, entonces si tenéis frío después de la procesión podéis venir a la plaza mayor para tomar un chocolate caliente.

Put a cross [×] in each one of the **three** correct boxes.

The article says ...

☐ A some roads will be closed all day.		☐ D you should park in the town centre.
☐ B there is a festival taking place soon.		☐ E you can go to the square to warm up.
☐ C the religious event is on Thursday.		☐ F hot drinks will be served.

(3 marks)

School

6 Read David's comments about his school.

> Llegamos a vivir al pueblo en junio por lo que soy nuevo en el colegio. Este es mi tercer mes como estudiante aquí.
>
> En mi antiguo instituto, la asignatura que me gustaba más eran las matemáticas, pero aquí las clases son un poco difíciles de seguir. Las que más disfruto ahora son las de dibujo.
>
> Mi profesora favorita es una mujer inglesa que nos da clases de ciencias. Es muy divertida y nos hace reír mucho.

Complete the gap in each sentence using a word or phrase from the box below.

There are more words / phrases than gaps.

> since July   three months   a week
> Maths   Art   English   Science

(a) David has been at the school ....

(b) The subject he enjoys most is ....

(c) His favourite teacher teaches ....

(3 marks)

My town

7 Read Indra's blog about her town.

> Me encanta mi pueblo y he vivido aquí toda mi vida, pero sé que hay cosas que tenemos que cambiar. Aquí voy a hablar de lo bueno y lo malo del pueblo.
>
> Primero quiero dar las gracias a la gente que limpia las calles. Hace un trabajo excelente y nuestro pueblo nunca está sucio.
>
> Creo que necesitamos más zonas de juego para los niños, especialmente para los que viven en pisos y no tienen jardín. Hay sitio para un nuevo parque detrás del supermercado.
>
> Los autobuses que van a la ciudad son modernos y cómodos, pero solo hay dos al día. Hay mucha gente mayor que necesita un servicio más frecuente.
>
> Estoy muy **preocupada** por el número de accidentes que hay en las calles cerca del instituto. Con todos los coches, es ahora una zona peligrosa.

See this photo in colour

(a) Complete the sentences below. Put a cross [×] in the correct box for each question.

(i) Indra's blog about the town points out ...

☐ A	the positive aspects.
☐ B	the negative side.
☐ C	both the good and the bad.

(ii) Indra ...

☐ A	complains about litter.
☐ B	thinks the town is clean.
☐ C	has been litter-picking.

Had a go ☐ **Nearly there** ☐ **Nailed it!** ☐

Practice papers

(iii) Indra thinks they need more …

☐ **A** play areas.
☐ **B** flats.
☐ **C** gardens.

(iv) Indra says that the buses …

☐ **A** are old and dirty.
☐ **B** never run on time.
☐ **C** are not frequent enough.

(b) Which of these is the best translation for the word *preocupada*?

Put a cross [×] in the correct box.

☐ **A** pleased
☐ **B** worried
☐ **C** busy

(5 marks)

Advice for shoppers

8 Read the shopping advice in this online article.

> No tienes que comprar todo en el supermercado. Puedes ir al mercado al final del día porque entonces a menudo venden verduras y fruta a precios muy buenos.
>
> Recomiendo comer algo antes de ir – no debes tener hambre cuando haces la compra. Siempre mira cuánto cuestan los productos – las marcas famosas son más caras y no siempre mejores.

(a) Complete the gap in each sentence using a word or phrase from the box below.
There are more words / phrases than gaps.

> supermarket   market   fruit and vegetable shop
> compare prices   find special offers   write a list   eat something

(i) The article points out the benefits of going to the ……………………………… . **(1 mark)**

(ii) Before you shop, you should ……………………………… . **(1 mark)**

(iii) You should always ……………………………… . **(1 mark)**

The article continues with further advice.

> Cuando estás buscando un producto, muchas veces ponen las cosas más caras donde tu mano llega fácilmente. Hay que mirar arriba y abajo. Recomiendo leer la información en los productos, especialmente si estás intentando comprar la comida más sana. Tendrás una sorpresa si miras la cantidad de sal o azúcar que hay en la comida. Esto es especialmente verdad cuando es comida preparada. Por esta razón, siempre es mejor comprar ingredientes naturales.

(b) Complete the sentences. Put a cross [×] in the correct box for each question.

(i) The more expensive products are placed …

☐ **A** within easy reach.
☐ **B** near the entrance.
☐ **C** by the tills.

(ii) You should read the product information if you want …

☐ **A** the best value.
☐ **B** the healthier options.
☐ **C** to check the sell-by date.

(2 marks)

Practice papers   Had a go ☐   Nearly there ☐   Nailed it! ☐

(c) Answer the following questions **in English**. You do not need to write in full sentences.

(i) What information might surprise you? (**one** detail)

....

(1 mark)

(ii) What is it always best to do?

....

(1 mark)

(Total for Question 8 = 7 marks)

A new sports centre

9 Read these social media comments about a new sports centre.

> **Julia:** Yo uso silla de ruedas y este maravilloso centro de deportes tiene clases de natación para las personas con discapacidad. El único problema es que no hay muchos sitios donde se pueda dejar el coche.
>
> **Omar:** El aspecto que más me gusta es el bar con vistas a la piscina. Puedo tomar un café mientras miro a mis hijos en el agua. Creo que sería mejor subir un poco la temperatura del agua – mis hijos dicen que está muy fría.
>
> **Carmen:** Esta semana fui a mi primera clase de baile moderno. La profesora es increíble y los estudiantes son gente muy simpática. Lo único que no me gusta es la hora a la que comienzan las clases. Sería mejor comenzar más temprano.

Complete the tables **in English**. You do not need to write in full sentences.

(a)
Reason Julia likes the centre	
The one problem with it	

(b)
Reason Omar likes the bar	
What he recommends	

(c)
What Carmen did this week	
What she would change	

(6 marks)

Studying

10 Translate the following sentences **into English**.

(a) Espero continuar con mis estudios.

....

(b) Quiero un trabajo durante las vacaciones de verano.

....

(c) Tuvimos una fiesta después de los exámenes.

....

(d) Mi primo está estudiando en el extranjero para un año.

....

(e) Me gustaría aprender a tocar un instrumento musical.

....

(10 marks)

TOTAL FOR PAPER = 50 MARKS

Had a go ☐ Nearly there ☐ Nailed it! ☐

Practice papers

Paper 4: Writing (Foundation)

In the real exam, you will write your answers on the question paper. Here, some lines are provided but you may need to write the rest of your answer on your own paper.

Picture-based task

1 Describe the photo. Write four short sentences **in Spanish**.

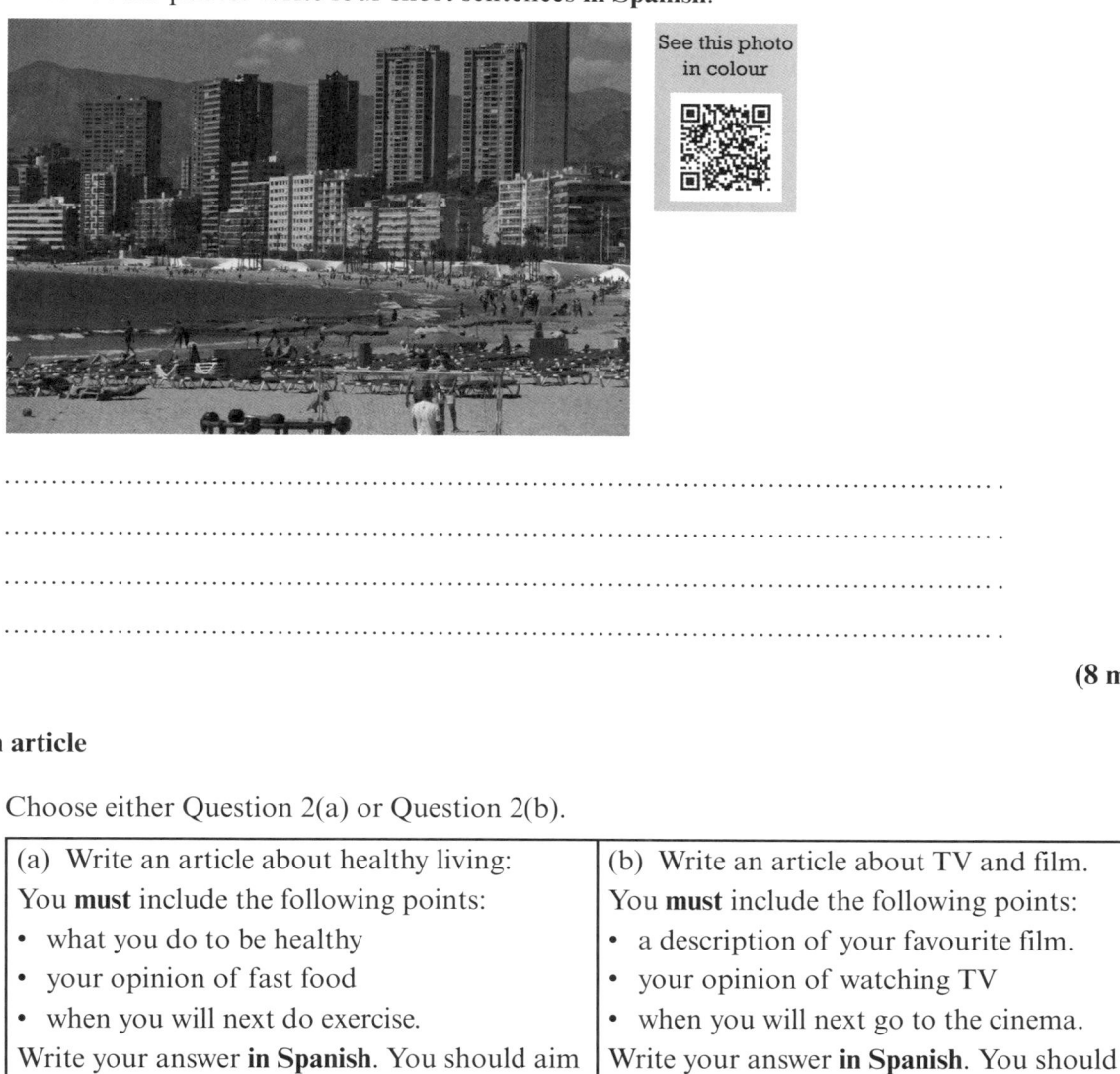

See this photo in colour

....
....
....
....

(8 marks)

An article

2 Choose either Question 2(a) or Question 2(b).

(a) Write an article about healthy living: You **must** include the following points: • what you do to be healthy • your opinion of fast food • when you will next do exercise. Write your answer **in Spanish**. You should aim to write between 40 and 50 words. **(14 marks)**	(b) Write an article about TV and film. You **must** include the following points: • a description of your favourite film. • your opinion of watching TV • when you will next go to the cinema. Write your answer **in Spanish**. You should aim to write between 40 and 50 words. **(14 marks)**

....
....
....
....
....
....

Practice papers

Had a go ☐   Nearly there ☐   Nailed it! ☐

A letter

3 Choose either Question 3(a) or Question 3(b).

| (a) Write a letter to your friend about your school holidays. You **must** include the following points:
• what you like to do during the summer holidays
• your opinion of having homework during holidays
• what you did last winter in the holidays
• where you want to travel in future.
Write your answer **in Spanish**. You should aim to write between 80 and 90 words.
(18 marks) | (b) Write a letter to your friend about food and drink.
You **must** include the following points:
• when you usually have meals
• your opinion of Spanish food
• what you prepared to eat at home last week
• where you will eat out in the future.
Write your answer **in Spanish**. You should aim to write between 80 and 90 words.
(18 marks) |

....
....
....
....
....
....

Translation

4 Translate the following five sentences **into Spanish**.

(a) I am sixteen and I am tall.

....

(b) My birthday is the second of July.

....

(c) My house is not far from the town.

....

(d) Normally I get up at half past seven in the morning.

....

(e) Yesterday I made a cake for my grandmother.

....

(10 marks)

TOTAL FOR PAPER = 50 MARKS

Had a go ☐   Nearly there ☐   Nailed it! ☐

Practice papers

Paper 1: Speaking (Higher)

Pearson Edexcel publishes official Sample Assessment Material on its website. This test has been written to help you practise what you have learned across the four skills and may not be representative of a real exam paper.

Read aloud

Media and technology

1   Javier, your friend, has written about social media. Read out the text below.

> Uso las redes sociales de vez en cuando para subir fotos o bajar música.
> Utilizo mi móvil bastante. Llamo a mis amigos, busco información y me gustan los juegos que hay.
> Aunque la pantalla es pequeña, es posible ver películas, y algunos de los vídeos en línea son muy divertidos.

Now listen to a recording of two questions related to what you have read.

You are expected to say a few words or a short phrase / sentence in response to each question. One-word answers will not be sufficient to gain full marks.

(12 marks)

Track 119

Role play

2   **Setting: At a hotel**

Scenario: You are in a hotel wanting to book rooms for your family.

Listen to the recording of the teacher's part. The teacher will play the part of the hotel receptionist and will speak first. They will ask questions **in Spanish** and you must answer **in Spanish**. You are expected to say a few words or a short phrase / sentence in response to each prompt. One-word answers will not be sufficient to gain full marks.

Track 120

> **Task:**
> 1 Ask a question about rooms.
> 2 Say what sort of rooms you want.
> 3 Say how long you will be staying.
> 4 Give your opinion about the area.
> 5 Ask a question about meals.

(10 marks)

Practice papers

Had a go ☐ Nearly there ☐ Nailed it! ☐

Picture-based task

Picture 1

Picture 2

3 Describe **ONE** of these pictures. You will tell your teacher which one you have chosen to describe.

Your description must cover:

- people
- location
- activity.

When you have finished your description, play the recording to hear and answer two questions relating to your chosen picture.

You are expected to say a few words or a short phrase / sentence in response to each question. One-word answers will not be sufficient to gain full marks.

(12 marks)

You will then move on to a conversation on the broader thematic context of **My neighbourhood.**

During the conversation, you will answer questions in the present, past and future tenses. Your responses should be as full and detailed as possible.

(16 marks)

TOTAL FOR PAPER = 50 MARKS

Had a go ☐   Nearly there ☐   Nailed it! ☐

Practice papers

Paper 2: Listening (Higher)

Sports

Track 123

1 David is talking about his favourite football player. What does he say? Listen to the recording and complete the sentences by putting a cross [×] in the correct box for each question.

(a) The footballer currently plays …

☐ A for an African team.
☐ B in Spain.
☐ C for his country.

(b) The player …

☐ A trains hard with the team.
☐ B is well respected by the fans.
☐ C is fast and very fit.

(c) In the last match, he …

☐ A was injured.
☐ B scored the winning goal.
☐ C could not play as he was ill.

(3 marks)

Holidays

Track 124

2 Lola is talking about the town where she goes on holiday. What does she say? Complete the gap in each sentence using a word or phrase from the box below. There are more words / phrases than gaps.

> countryside   sea   old town   city centre
> rents a flat   owns a house   stays on a campsite
> on the beach   reading   sunbathing   in the pool

(a) Tourists go mainly to the ……………………………………………………………………………….

(b) Some never go to the …………………………………………………………………………………..

(c) In the town, Lola ………………………………………………………………………………………..

(d) The children spend their time ……………………………………………………………………….

(e) The adults spend their time ………………………………………………………………………….

(5 marks)

Eating out

Track 125

3 Miguel is talking about a meal in a restaurant. What does he mention?
Listen to the recording and put a cross [×] in each one of the **three** correct boxes.

| ☐ A starters | ☐ C drinks | ☐ E desserts |
| ☐ B vegetarian options | ☐ D service | ☐ F cost |

(3 marks)

A healthy lifestyle

Track 126

4 Ana, Iván and Karima are talking about their lifestyles. What do they say?

Listen to the recording and complete the sentences by putting a cross [×] in the correct box for each question.

(a) Ana thinks she should …

☐ A try a team sport.
☐ B do more exercise.
☐ C get more sleep.

(b) She plans to …

☐ A do more walking.
☐ B eat more healthily.
☐ C get more fresh air.

131

Practice papers   Had a go ☐   Nearly there ☐   Nailed it! ☐

(c) Iván needs to stop …

☐	A	watching films too late.
☐	B	going on the internet at bedtime.
☐	C	reading when he should be asleep.

(d) Karima is going to …

☐	A	go to study sessions.
☐	B	attend a book club.
☐	C	start a new hobby.

(4 marks)

Jobs and money

Track 127

5 Toni, Leya and Jalil are talking about earning money. What do they say? Listen to the recording and complete the following tables **in English**. You do not need to write in full sentences.

(a)	Reason Toni needs money	
(b)	Why Lola does not spend her money	
(c)	Reason Jalil's parents said 'no' to the job	

(3 marks)

The environment

Track 128

6 Alex is talking about his experiences last year. What does he say? Complete the gap in each sentence using a word from the box below. There are more words than gaps.

> wettest   hottest   windiest
> sun   cloud   rain   cold

(a) Last year was one of the .... he can remember. **(1 mark)**

(b) When he went on holiday, they had .... most days and they were glad of the ....

(2 marks)

(Total for Question 6 = 3 marks)

Future opportunities

Track 129

7 Amira, Vicente and Marta are talking about the advantages and disadvantages of doing the Bachillerato* at school. What do they say? Listen to the recording and complete the following table **in English**. You do not need to write in full sentences.

Bachillerato – course for 16–18-year-olds, similar to A-levels

	Advantage	Disadvantage
(a) Amira		
(b) Vicente		
(c) Marta		

(6 marks)

Family and relationships

Track 130

8 Hugo and Karima are talking about family and relationships. What do they say? Listen to the recordings and complete the sentences by putting a cross [×] in the correct box for each question.

(a) Hugo

(i) Hugo's sister, María, …

☐	A	went to a university party.
☐	B	has just met a Cuban boy.
☐	C	has a long-term boyfriend.

(ii) Last night …

☐	A	María came home really angry.
☐	B	Hugo heard María crying.
☐	C	María went out for a meal.

(iii) Hugo thinks …

☐	A	his mum argued with María.
☐	B	María got a text that upset her.
☐	C	María and her boyfriend broke up.

Had a go ☐ **Nearly there** ☐ **Nailed it!** ☐

Practice papers

(3 marks)

(b) Karima

(i) Karima is unhappy at home because …

☐ A she does not get on with her parents.
☐ B the atmosphere is awful.
☐ C she is always fighting with her brother.

(ii) Karima's father …

☐ A owns his own company.
☐ B is having trouble at work.
☐ C has lost his job.

(iii) Karima's brother, Juan, …

☐ A is in trouble with the police.
☐ B does not intend to follow his father's wishes.
☐ C wants to be a film director.

(3 marks)

(Total for Question 8 = 6 marks)

Equality

Track 131

9 (a) Listen to Natalia's podcast about equality. What does she say?
Listen to the recording and put a cross [×] in each one of the **three** correct boxes.

☐ A The woman in the story was from Latin America.
☐ B She went into a designer clothes shop.
☐ C She was a famous singer.
☐ D The shop assistant did not recognise her.
☐ E The assistant assumed the customer was poor.
☐ F The assistant gave her a free gift.

(3 marks)

(b) Natalia now shares some information about the Equality Awareness Day they held in school. Listen to the recording and answer the following questions **in English**.
You do not need to write in full sentences.

(i) What were the visiting guests invited to do? ……………………………………………………… .

(ii) Who was the first guest? ……………………………………………………… .

(iii) What did she explain? ……………………………………………………… .

(iv) What did the second guest tell them about? ……………………………………………………… .

(4 marks)

(Total for Question 9 = 7 marks)

Dictation

Track 132

10 You are going to hear someone talking about tourist attractions. Sentences 1–2: write down the missing words in the gaps provided. In each gap, you will write one word **in Spanish**.

Example: Creo <u>que</u> el <u>puente</u> es muy <u>viejo</u>.

1 La ………………………. fue ………………………. en el último ………………………. .

2 El ………………………. ………………………. es muy ………………………. .

Sentences 3–6: write down the full sentences that you hear in the spaces provided, **in Spanish**.

Example: <u>Vamos a pasear en bicicleta.</u>

3 ……………………………………………………………………………………………………… .

4 ……………………………………………………………………………………………………… .

5 ……………………………………………………………………………………………………… .

6 ……………………………………………………………………………………………………… .

(10 marks)

TOTAL FOR PAPER = 50 MARKS

Paper 3: Reading (Higher)

School

1 Read David's comments about his school.

> Soy nuevo en el colegio porque solo vinimos a vivir al pueblo en junio. Este es mi tercer mes como estudiante allí.
>
> En mi antiguo instituto, la asignatura que me gustaba más eran las matemáticas, pero aquí las clases son un poco difíciles de seguir. Las que más disfruto ahora son las de dibujo.
>
> Mi profesora favorita es una mujer inglesa que nos da clases de ciencias. Es muy divertida y nos hace reír mucho.

Complete the gap in each sentence using a word or phrase from the box below. There are more words than gaps.

| since July | three months | a week |
| Maths | Art | English | Science |

(a) David has been at the school ....

(b) The subject he enjoys most is ....

(c) His favourite teacher teaches ....

(3 marks)

My town

2 Read Indra's blog about her town.

> Me encanta mi pueblo y he vivido aquí toda mi vida, pero sé que hay cosas que tenemos que cambiar. Aquí voy a hablar de lo bueno y lo malo del pueblo.
>
> Primero quiero dar las gracias a la gente que limpia las calles. Hace un trabajo excelente y nuestro pueblo nunca está sucio ni tiene basura.
>
> Creo que necesitamos más zonas de juego para los niños, especialmente para los que viven en pisos y no tienen jardín. Hay sitio para un nuevo parque detrás del supermercado.
>
> Los autobuses que van a la ciudad son modernos y cómodos, pero solo hay tres al día. Hay mucha gente mayor que necesita un servicio más frecuente.
>
> Estoy muy **preocupada** por el número de accidentes que hay en las calles cerca del instituto. Con todos los coches, es ahora una zona peligrosa.

See this photo in colour

(a) Complete the sentences below. Put a cross [×] in the correct box for each question.

(i) Indra's blog about the town points out …

☐ A the positive aspects.
☐ B the negative side.
☐ C both the good and the bad.

(ii) Indra …

☐ A complains about litter.
☐ B thinks the town is clean.
☐ C has been litter-picking.

(iii) Indra thinks they need more …

☐ A play areas.
☐ B flats.
☐ C gardens.

(iv) Indra says that the buses …

☐ A are old and dirty.
☐ B never run on time.
☐ C are not frequent enough.

(b) Which of these is the best translation for the word *preocupada*?

Put a cross [×] in the correct box.

☐ A pleased   ☐ B worried   ☐ C busy

(5 marks)

Had a go ☐ Nearly there ☐ Nailed it! ☐   **Practice papers**

Advice for shoppers

3 Read the shopping advice in this online article.

> No tienes que comprar todo en el supermercado. Puedes ir al mercado al final del día porque entonces a menudo venden verduras y fruta a precios muy buenos.
>
> Recomiendo comer algo antes de ir – no debes tener hambre cuando haces la compra. Siempre mira cuánto cuestan los productos; las marcas famosas son más caras y no siempre mejores.

(a) Complete the gap in each sentence using a word or sentence from the box below.

There are more words / sentences than gaps.

> supermarket   market   fruit and vegetable shop
> compare prices   find special offers   write a list   eat something

(i)   The article points out the benefits of going to the .... **(1 mark)**

(ii) Before you shop, you should .... **(1 mark)**

(iii) You should always .... **(1 mark)**

The article continues with further advice.

> Cuando estás buscando un producto, muchas veces ponen las cosas más caras donde tu mano puede llegar fácilmente. Hay que mirar arriba y abajo. Recomiendo leer la información en los productos, especialmente si estás intentando comprar la comida más sana. Tendrás una sorpresa si miras la cantidad de sal o azúcar que hay en la comida. Esto es especialmente verdad cuando es comida preparada. Por esta razón, siempre es mejor comprar ingredientes naturales.

(b) Complete the sentences. Put a cross [×] in the correct box for each question.

(i) The more expensive products are placed …

☐ A within easy reach.
☐ B near the entrance.
☐ C by the tills.

(ii) You should read the product information if you want …

☐ A the best value.
☐ B the healthier options.
☐ C to check the sell-by date.

(2 marks)

(c) Answer the following questions **in English**. You do not need to write in full sentences.

(i) What information might surprise you? (**one** detail) .... **(1 mark)**

(ii) What is it always best to do? .... **(1 mark)**

(Total for Question 3 = 7 marks)

A holiday home website

4 Read this review of a holiday home website.

> El sitio web es muy útil y las fotos muestran imágenes muy claras de las casas. Es un poco irritante que no muestre exactamente dónde están las casas, pero entiendo que es para proteger a los *propietarios*. ¡No querrán que las personas curiosas vengan a mirar por las ventanas!

(a) Answer the following questions **in English**. You do not need to write in full sentences.

(i) What was good about the photos? .... **(1 mark)**

(ii) Why was the reviewer irritated by the website? .... **(1 mark)**

(b) Which of these is the best translation of the word *propietarios*?

Put a cross [×] in the correct box.

| ☐ A buyers | ☐ B owners | ☐ C expenses |

(1 mark)

(Total for Question 4 = 3 marks)

Travel problems

5 Read Leya's and Iván's blogs about travel problems they have had.

> **Leya:**
> Fui de Madrid a las Islas Canarias para pasar unas semanas con mi tía. Le dije que iba a llegar a las diez de la mañana. Pero me olvidé de que hay una diferencia de una hora entre España y allí. Antes de salir del avión, saqué mi móvil para explicarle la hora de llegada correcta, pero se quedó sin batería. Cuando llegué al aeropuerto, tuve que pasar una hora en el café esperando a mi tía.

(a) Put a cross [×] next to each one of the **three** correct statements.

☐	A	Leya's aunt lives in the Canary Islands.
☐	B	Leya said she would arrive at ten.
☐	C	She forgot there was a time difference.
☐	D	She managed to text her aunt.
☐	E	She left her phone on the plane.
☐	F	Her aunt had to wait ages for her to arrive.

(3 marks)

> **Iván**
> Estaba de vacaciones en Europa con mi familia y un día fuimos de excursión. Durante el día, vimos algunos de los sitios más bonitos de la región. Sin embargo, tuvimos que pasar demasiado tiempo en el autobús. Hacía mucho calor y no podíamos abrir las ventanas. Lo peor fue cuando el autobús paró al cruzar la frontera entre dos países y tardaron un montón en comprobar los pasaportes.

(b) What does Iván tell us? Complete the tables **in English**. You do not need to write in full sentences.

(i)	What they saw during the trip	
(ii)	The reason it was uncomfortable on the bus (one detail)	
(iii)	The reason the bus stopped	
(iv)	Why there was a delay	

(4 marks)

(Total for Question 5 = 7 marks)

The natural world

6 Read this extract from the website of a nature reserve.

> En nuestra reserva encontrarás ejemplos de muchos tipos de hábitat desde tierra seca hasta lagos y valles. Aquí verás pájaros y otras especies que descansan allí antes de continuar su viaje al sur para el invierno.
>
> La gente que nos visita recomienda empezar en el centro educativo donde hay una lista de los pájaros que hemos visto en la reserva esa semana. Así puedes tener una buena idea de lo que podrías ver en la reserva.

See this photo in colour

Had a go ☐ **Nearly there** ☐ **Nailed it!** ☐   **Practice papers**

(a) Put a cross [×] next to each one of the **two** correct statements.

☐	**A** The park is in a mountainous region.
☐	**B** Some birds pause there on their way south.
☐	**C** It is best to begin in the visitors' centre.
☐	**D** You never know what you might see on the reserve.

(2 marks)

The website provides further information.

> Aunque hay una gran zona para dejar los coches, recomendamos venir en tren porque hay una estación a un cuarto de hora andando. Si presentas el billete de tren, te cobramos dos euros menos para entrar.
>
> En los jardines hay mesas y sillas para tomar el almuerzo si traes comida de casa. O puedes disfrutar de una variedad de platos fríos y calientes servidos en nuestro restaurante.
>
> Los pequeños pueden divertirse en el parque de niños o subirse a los árboles en el bosque con la supervisión de sus padres (¡claro!).

(b) What does the information tell us? Complete the tables **in English**. You do not need to write in full sentences.

(i)	Why it is worth travelling by train	
(ii)	What the restaurant provides	
(iii)	What the children can do in the wood	

(3 marks)

(Total for Question 6 = 5 marks)

My favourite novel

7 Read Rosalía's review of a novel.

> Leí esta novela por primera vez cuando tenía diecisiete años y, a menudo, las opiniones cambian con el tiempo. Pero cuando la leí otra vez la semana pasada me gustó tanto como antes. Reconozco que es una novela larguísima, de unas cuatrocientas páginas, y que no es una historia fácil para pasar un rato* en la playa en verano. Esta novela requiere tiempo y dedicación, ¡pero vale la pena!
>
> El libro cuenta la historia de Alba, una chica nueva en un instituto privado que está lleno de los hijos y las hijas de gente muy rica. Ella también parece ser de una familia con dinero, pero está escondiendo un secreto. Es, en realidad, la hija de una de las mujeres que limpia el colegio y le han dado a Alba una plaza gratis en el instituto.

rato – while, time

(a) Complete the sentences below.

Put a cross [×] in the correct box for each question.

(i) Rosalía says she …

☐	**A** likes the book as much as ever.
☐	**B** preferred the book when she was younger.
☐	**C** appreciates the book more now.

(ii) Rosalía warns people that the novel …

☐	**A** contains upsetting themes.
☐	**B** will make you laugh out loud.
☐	**C** is extremely long.

(iii) She describes it as …

☐	**A** a fun summer read.
☐	**B** worth the effort.
☐	**C** a book you will not forget.

(3 marks)

(b) Answer the following questions **in English**. You do not need to write in full sentences.

(i) Who are the typical students at the school? .... **(1 mark)**

(ii) What is the character Alba's secret? .... **(1 mark)**

(Total for Question 7 = 5 marks)

Practice papers

Had a go ☐ Nearly there ☐ Nailed it! ☐

Interview feedback

8 Read the comments that Mario received from the boss, Sara Martínez, after his interview.

> Estimado Mario
>
> Gracias por asistir a la entrevista el lunes pasado. Tengo que informarte de que, a pesar de ser un candidato muy fuerte, no hemos podido darte el trabajo. Lo siento.
>
> Aquí te ofrezco un comentario sobre lo bueno de tu entrevista y mis consejos sobre las cosas que puedes hacer para mejorar en el futuro.
>
> Llegaste con tiempo y vestido adecuadamente para una entrevista formal. Te presentaste como simpático y abierto, y tuve la impresión de que te llevarías bien con los otros compañeros en el equipo.
>
> Cuando te hice preguntas, no parecías saber mucho de la empresa ni del trabajo que hacemos. Es muy importante buscar información sobre la compañía antes de la entrevista. Una pregunta típica es siempre '¿Por qué quieres el trabajo?', y si no entiendes la función de la empresa, no podrás contestar.
>
> Tus primeras dos preguntas se trataron de las vacaciones y el pago. Esto no da una buena impresión. Los empresarios necesitan creer que lo que te interesa más es el empleo.
>
> Atentamente
>
> *Sara Martínez*
>
> Jefa de ventas

Answer the following questions **in English**. You do not need to write in full sentences.

(a) What news does Mario find out at the start of the letter? ....

(b) What advice does Sara say she will give him? ....

(c) How did Sara feel Mario would fit in at work? ....

(d) What impression did Mario give when Sara asked him questions? ....

(e) Why did Mario give a bad impression when he asked questions? ....

(5 marks)

My free time

9 Translate the following passage **into English**.

> Me gusta mucho hacer ejercicio físico y cada día salgo a correr por el gran parque en la ciudad. A menudo preparo platos vegetarianos para la familia. También me relajo escuchando música. Mi hermano se parece mucho a mi padre y los dos son muy aficionados al baloncesto. Fueron a ver un partido ayer.

....

....

....

....

....

....

....

....

(9 marks)

TOTAL FOR PAPER = 50 MARKS

Had a go ☐ Nearly there ☐ Nailed it! ☐

Practice papers

Paper 4: Writing (Higher)

In the real exam, you will write your answers on the question paper. Here, some lines are provided but you may need to write the rest of your answer on your own paper.

A letter

1 Choose either Question 1(a) or Question 1(b).

| (a) Write a letter to your friend about your school holidays:
You **must** include the following points:
• what you like to do during the summer holidays
• your opinion of having homework during holidays
• what you did last winter in the holidays
• where you want to travel in future.
Write your answer **in Spanish**. You should aim to write between 80 and 90 words.
(18 marks) | (b) Write a letter to your friend about food and drink.
You **must** include the following points:
• when you usually have meals
• your opinion of Spanish food
• what you prepared to eat at home last week
• where you will eat out in the future.
Write your answer in Spanish. You should aim to write between 80 and 90 words.
(18 marks) |

....
....
....
....
....
....
....
....
....

Practice papers

Had a go ☐ Nearly there ☐ Nailed it! ☐

A blog

2 Choose either Question 2(a) or Question 2(b).

| (a) Write a blog about friends and family.
You **must** include the following points:
• what makes a good friend
• the pros and cons of going out with a group of friends
• a night out that you had with friends in the past
• what you and your family are going to do next weekend.
Write your answer in Spanish. You should aim to write between 130 and 150 words.
(22 marks) | (b) Write a blog about life at school.
You **must** include the following points:
• the best lesson you have at school
• the pros and cons of school rules
• what your first day at school was like
• what different subjects students should study at school.
Write your answer in Spanish. You should aim to write between 130 and 150 words.
(22 marks) |

Translation

3 Translate the paragraph **into Spanish**.

> Every year I go to a small town on the coast in the east of Spain. There are lots of tourists there and the atmosphere is very pleasant. It is usually very hot and sunny, especially in the afternoon. However, last August we had two days of rain. We will go back this summer too.

(10 marks)

TOTAL FOR PAPER = 50 MARKS

Answers

1. Introducing yourself
1   B, D, E
2   (a) summer   (b) north   (c) winter

2. Physical descriptions
1   (a) Most students have brown hair.
     (b) There are three fair-haired students.
     (c) Only one student has red hair.
     (d) The students with fair hair have blue or grey eyes.
     (e) A total of seven students wear glasses.

2

	Likes	Dislikes
(a)	height / being tall	glasses
(b)	eyes	nose
(c)	arms	nose
(d)	legs	mouth

3. Character descriptions
1

	Who …	Luis	Marta	Nadim	Sara
(a)	… is the most helpful?			×	
(b)	… is the youngest?				×
(c)	… always gets tired?		×		
(d)	… is the natural leader?	×			
(e)	… has a positive outlook?				×
(f)	… is the sporty one?		×		

2   ¿Cómo es mi personalidad? Bueno / Pues, creo que soy simpático/a y divertido/a, con una actitud positiva y optimista. Soy bastante trabajador/a y responsable. No soy muy deportista, pero soy alegre. Mis amigos dicen que soy listo/a, pero estoy nervioso/a cuando tengo exámenes.

4. Family
1   B, C, F
2   Sample answer:
En la foto hay once personas; creo que todos son miembros de la misma familia. Están los abuelos, los padres y los hijos. Están en la cocina de una casa y en la mesa hay comida, fruta y vasos. En mi opinión, es una celebración, como un cumpleaños, por ejemplo. Todos están muy contentos y alegres.

Sample answers to follow-on questions:
(a) Mi familia no es muy numerosa, somos cuatro en total. Vivo con mi padre, mi madrastra y mi hermano mayor. Mi padre es alto y tiene el pelo corto y negro. Es divertido, pero estricto a veces. Mi madrastra es baja y bonita con el pelo marrón y los ojos grises. Es alegre y simpática. Mi hermano mayor tiene dieciocho años. Tiene el pelo marrón y bastante largo. Es muy deportista y trabajador.
(b) Me parezco bastante a mi hermano. Todo el mundo sabe que somos hermanos, pero yo no soy nada deportista.

5. What makes a good friend
1   Sample answers to follow-on questions:
     (a) Mi mejor amiga siempre está ahí cuando la necesito. Es simpática y tenemos mucho en común. Me escucha y me acepta, pero está dispuesta a decirme la verdad.

 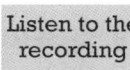 

     (b) Compartimos los mismos intereses en música y vamos a conciertos juntas. Es una chica simpática que me hace reír todo el tiempo.
2   (a) My best friend / helps me a lot.
     (b) I like to think that / I am a good friend.
     (c) A perfect friend always / accepts you as you are.
     (d) Friendship is very important / for young people.
     (e) There are moments / times when your friend / needs to tell you the truth.

6. Relationships (family and friends)
1

	Who …	Luisa	Amira	Diego
(a)	… wants more freedom?		×	
(b)	… needs their own space?			×
(c)	… used to fight a lot?	×		
(d)	… is always arguing?			×
(e)	… was protected at school?	×		
(f)	… thinks their parents are unfair?		×	

2   Sample answer:
Me llevo bien con mis amigos porque tenemos mucho en común. Son divertidos y simpáticos. A veces discutimos si queremos hacer cosas diferentes o queremos ir a sitios nuevos. Este fin de semana vamos a ir al centro comercial el sábado y vamos a ir a la piscina el domingo.

7. Helping a friend
1   1   Mi **mejor** amigo **siempre** me **ayuda**.
     2   Mis **compañeros** de **clase** me **evitaron**.
     3   Su comportamiento hacia nosotros cambió mucho.
     4   La amistad es muy importante cuando eres joven.
     5   Intenté olvidar el error.
     6   Tienes que dejar de fumar ahora.
2   Sample answer:
Hay dos personas en la foto, un chico con el pelo corto y marrón y una chica con el pelo largo y marrón. El chico lleva una camisa azul y blanca y la chica lleva una camiseta azul.

Creo que son estudiantes y pienso que están en el instituto o la cafetería de la universidad. Están hablando de sus estudios y mirando una tableta. En mi opinión, el chico tiene un problema con su trabajo y la chica le está ayudando.
Sample answers to follow-on questions:
(a) Un buen amigo es simpático y divertido. Escucha tus problemas.
(b) Vamos al cine y a veces jugamos en el parque.

8. Everyday life
1   (a) B   (b) C   (c) A
2   (a) Como mi desayuno en la cocina.
     (b) Normalmente me levanto a las ocho.
     (c) Sale de (la) casa y coge el autobús.
     (d) Hago mis deberes después de la cena.
     (e) El fin de semana pasado vi la televisión con mi familia.

9. Meals at home
1   (a) at different times   (b) her grandmother
     (c) she refuses to eat / won't eat her greens / the vegetables
     (d) a lighter meal
2   (a) I have a snack when I come back from school.
     (b) I take a sandwich to school to eat during break.
     (c) Yesterday we had dinner / the evening meal at around ten.

(d) This Sunday we are going to prepare / make lunch for my grandparents.
(e) At weekends I like to help cook / I like helping to cook.

10. Celebrations
1 1 **Organizamos** una fiesta de **cumpleaños**.
   2 **Cenamos** en un **restaurante**.
   3 Voy a **sacar** muchas **fotos**.
   4 Recibió camisetas y libros.
   5 Hice un pastel bastante grande.
   6 Fue una noche muy emocionante.
2 Sample answers:
   1 Es el cumpleaños del padre.
   2 Está abriendo sus regalos.
   3 El padre está con sus tres hijos.
   4 Hay tarjetas y un pastel sobre la mesa.

11. Food and drink
1 (a) B   (b) C   (c) B   (d) C
2 Sample answer:
Mi comida favorita es la pasta con queso, pero también me gustan las hamburguesas con patatas fritas. No me interesan mucho los postres.
El sábado pasado preparé una paella en casa para mi familia. Me gustó bastante, pero creo que necesitaba cocinar el arroz un poco más.
Para el cumpleaños de mi madre, la semana que viene, voy a hacer un gran pastel de chocolate. Es su favorito. Además, vamos a hacer unas tapas para la cena, algunas con carne y otras con pescado.

12. Healthy diets
1 Sample answer:
En la foto hay una familia a la mesa en la cocina. Están los abuelos, los padres y su hija. Están tomando una ensalada y pasta para la comida.
La abuela está hablando con la madre y la niña está poniendo ensalada en su plato. Es una comida muy sana.

Sample answers to follow-on questions:
(a) Una dieta sana es una dieta equilibrada con una variedad de comida diferente. Por ejemplo, carne, pescado, frutas, verduras, queso o leche y pasta o arroz.
(b) La comida basura como hamburguesas y patatas fritas, o cosas muy dulces con mucho azúcar, como pasteles, chocolate o churros.
2 Sample answers to follow-on questions:
(a) Me gusta preparar pasta porque es muy fácil y rápido.
(b) Voy a comer comida mexicana. ¡Me encanta!

13. Sport and exercise
1 (a) Lucía
Advantage: it's good / excellent for keeping fit
Disadvantage: (it's annoying when there are) too many people in the pool
(b) Mario
Advantage: spending time outdoors / in the open air
Disadvantage: it's not very comfortable when it rains
(c) Sara
Advantage: being a member of a team
Disadvantage: having to practise / train three times a week
2 T: Hola. ¿En qué puedo ayudarle?
S: Hola. Quiero entradas para el partido de baloncesto, por favor.
T: Muy bien. ¿Qué día es el partido?
S: Es el jueves de la semana que viene.
T: Ah sí. ¿Cuántas quiere?
S: Cuatro en total.

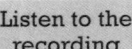 

T: Vale. ¿Te gusta el baloncesto entonces?
S: Sí, me gusta mucho, es muy emocionante.
T: Me alegro.
S: ¿Cuánto es en total?

14. Physical wellbeing
1 Sample answer:
En la foto hay un hombre joven en la cama. Son las dos menos veinte de la mañana, pero no duerme. Está mirando su móvil y podría estar chateando con alguien o buscando información en internet. No es buena idea usar la tecnología antes de dormirte porque te despierta más. Creo que el chico va a estar muy cansado por la mañana.

Sample answers to follow-on questions:
(a) Creo que como una dieta equilibrada, bebo suficiente agua y duermo bien.
(b) El fin de semana pasado, fui a pasear en el bosque con mi perro.
2 (a) Mi hermano duerme muy bien cada noche / todas las noches.
   (b) Me gusta pasar tiempo al aire libre.
   (c) Bebí mucha agua ayer.
   (d) El sol puede hacer daño a tu piel / a la piel.
   (e) Está muy cansada hoy.

15. Mental wellbeing
1 (a) A   (b) A   (c) C   (d) B   (e) C   (f) B
2 (a) I like painting because it's very relaxing.
   (b) My grandfather always listens to me if I have a problem.
   (c) When I feel sad / upset, I talk to my friends.
   (d) I helped my brother when he had a problem.
   (e) Family relationships are very important for mental health.

16. Feeling unwell
1 T: ¿Cuál es el problema?
S: Me duele la rodilla.
T: Y ¿qué pasó?
S: Estaba paseando en bicicleta cuando me caí y me hice daño en la rodilla.
T: ¿Cuánto tiempo vas a estar aquí en España?
S: Vamos a estar una semana más.
T: Y ¿cuándo volvéis a casa?
S: El sábado próximo.
T: Vale. Vas a necesitar tomar una medicina.
S: ¿Cuándo abren la farmacia?
T: A las ocho.
2 El año pasado cuando fuimos a España, tuve un accidente. Estaba bajando la escalera en el hotel el último día de las vacaciones y me caí. Me dolía mucho el brazo y fui al doctor. Me dijo que el brazo estaba roto. Tuve que ir al hospital.

17. Role models in sport
1 (a) She was the first female referee in a World Cup match in men's football.
   (b) The line judges / assistant referees were also women.
   (c) B Brazilian
   (d) Girls were not allowed to play football.
   (e) B She thinks there is still some way to go.
2 Me llamo Paula y este año soy capitana del equipo de fútbol de mi instituto. Me encanta el deporte porque me ayuda a mantenerme en forma y disfruto la amistad con los miembros del equipo. La semana pasada ganamos el partido, pero este sábado creo que perderemos / vamos a perder contra un equipo muy bueno.

18. Sporting events
1 (a) Sara
Opinion: Didn't enjoy themselves
Reason: (One of the following) It was raining / They were cold
(b) Vicente
Opinion: Marvellous / great / wonderful experience
Reason: Atmosphere was exciting

(c) Lola
Opinion: Had a pleasant afternoon
Reason: Brother won several races
2 Sample answer:
En la foto hay cuatro personas, dos chicos y dos chicas. Están en la sala de la casa y están viendo un partido de fútbol en la televisión. Creo que el partido es muy emocionante y su equipo está ganando porque los chicos están muy felices.
Sample answers to follow-on questions:
(a) Nunca voy a ver partidos en persona. La verdad es que no me interesa mucho el deporte, pero a mi familia le encanta.
(b) Ellos ven todo tipo de deporte en la tele y, a menudo, mi hermano va con mi padre a ver partidos de fútbol en el estadio.

19. Me and my mobile
1 1 Hay cuatro chicos en la foto.
   2 Todos tienen un móvil.
   3 Dos de los jóvenes escuchan música en el móvil.
   4 La chica a la izquierda muestra una foto a su amigo.
2 1 Esta **aplicación** es muy **útil**.
   2 Los **juegos** son bastante **divertidos**.
   3 Vas a **romper** la **pantalla**.
   4 Vamos a enviar unas fotos.
   5 Mando mensajes a mis amigos.
   6 Descargo vídeos y canciones.

20. Social media
1 (a) meet new people
   (b) find a partner
   (c) the fun things
   (d) the hurtful comments
   (e) the privacy issues
2 Read aloud text

21. The internet
1 (a) B (b) C (c) A
2 (a) She likes to make the holiday experience last.
   (b) check the weather (in the country she is going to)
   (c) makes a list of places to visit
   (d) a presentation with photos and comments
   (e) She likes to have a souvenir of the trip.

22. Computer games
1 T: Buenos días. ¿En qué puedo ayudarle?
   S: Quiero comprar un videojuego.
   T: ¿Para quién es?
   S: Es para mi hermana.
   T: ¿Qué tipo de juego prefiere?
   S: Me gustaría un juego de aventura.
   T: ¿Qué piensa usted de los videojuegos?
   S: No me gustan mucho. Creo que son un poco aburridos.
   T: Vale.
   S: ¿Cuánto es este juego?
   T: Este juego cuesta quince euros.
2 (a) B (b) A (c) C (d) A

23. The good and bad of technology
1 Sample answer:
En la foto hay un hombre con un portátil. El hombre tiene el pelo corto y marrón y lleva una camiseta gris. Creo que está en su casa, o en su oficina no estoy seguro. Está mirando la pantalla de su portátil con terror porque algo malo ha pasado. Pienso que el ordenador va muy lento, o ha perdido su trabajo, y está muy enfadado.
Sample answers to follow-on questions:
(a) Me parece muy útil. Nos permite hacer muchas cosas y nos da acceso a mucha información. No sé qué haría sin Internet.
(b) Lo usé para ayudar con mis estudios, para bajar música y para ver las noticias sobre mis grupos favoritos.
2 Sample answer:
Normalmente uso Internet para mirar los sitios web de mis artistas favoritos y ver vídeos de los cantantes que me gustan. Creo que la tecnología es increíble y muy útil. Es perfecta para mantenerte en contacto con la familia y los amigos, y tiene muchos usos diferentes.
La semana pasada tuve un problema cuando estaba volviendo a casa tarde y no pude llamar a mis padres con el móvil porque me quedé sin batería*.
Este fin de semana voy a subir unas fotos de mis vacaciones y mandaré mis deberes a mi profesor de historia por correo electrónico.
*me quedé sin batería = I ran out of battery

24. Hobbies
1 1 Me **gusta** mucho el **dibujo**.
   2 A **veces** voy al **cine**.
   3 Ver la **televisión** es **aburrido**.
   4 Soy aficionado a las obras extranjeras.
   5 Prefiero las actividades artísticas.
   6 Me interesa la lectura.
2 Sample answers for follow-on questions:
   (a) Mis actividades favoritas son los deportes y actividades activas. El deporte que me gusta más es el fútbol y soy capitana del equipo de chicas en mi pueblo. También me gusta correr y, de vez en cuando, juego al tenis con mi hermana.
   (b) Juego al fútbol los miércoles por la tarde en las clases de educación física, y también con el equipo los sábados. Me voy a correr los domingos por la mañana. Solo jugamos al tenis en verano cuando hace buen tiempo.

25. Music and dance
1 (a) B (b) C (c) A (d) A (e) B (f) B
2 Sample answer:
La música que me gusta más es la música pop porque es alegre y perfecta para bailar. Escucho música cuando estoy en mi dormitorio o cuando estoy haciendo mis deberes. Me gustaría mucho ver un concierto de Taylor Swift porque canta muy bien y me encanta su voz.

26. Music and dance events
1 (a) B (b) A (c) C (d) B
2 (a) I have (got) the tickets for the concert.
   (b) I believe it is going to be very exciting.
   (c) My favourite group will play their latest songs.
   (d) Yesterday I listened to their music and read the words / lyrics.
   (e) We are going to have a very / really good time, I am sure.

27. Reading
1 Sample answer:
La foto es de un chico con el pelo marrón y rizado*. Lleva una camiseta blanca y una camisa azul. Tiene unos dieciocho años, creo. Podría ser la cocina de su casa. Está sentado a la mesa, y está leyendo una novela. Hay un vaso de agua. El chico tiene la boca abierta y creo que está muy sorprendido.
Pienso que había una gran sorpresa en el libro que está leyendo o que es una historia de terror y el chico tiene miedo.
*If you know vocabulary that is not on the prescribed list, you can use it. For example, here *rizado* (curly) is used successfully.
Sample answers for follow-on questions:
(a) Me gusta bastante. Cuando era pequeño, me encantaba leer, pero ahora es difícil encontrar tiempo. Y, claro, siempre hay muchas otras cosas que se pueden hacer.

(b) Leí una novela sobre una chica que descubre, a los dieciocho años, que tiene poderes especiales. Poco a poco aprende que no está sola y que hay otros como ella. Me gustó mucho porque fue emocionante y el personaje principal me hacía reír.
2. (a) No me gusta leer comedias.
   (b) Este libro tiene demasiadas páginas.
   (c) El personaje principal es muy simpático.
   (d) Mi hermano prefiere las novelas de ciencia ficción.
   (e) La semana pasada leí un libro con un final muy triste.

28. Television
1 Sample answer:
Me gusta ver las series de comedia o las películas de acción. Nunca veo los programas de cocina, no me interesan nada, y no veo las noticias mucho porque son tristes. Soy aficionado al deporte y más que nada me gusta ver los partidos de fútbol porque siempre son divertidos y emocionantes. La semana pasada vi un programa sobre los animales y la naturaleza. Fue muy educativo. Este fin de semana voy a ver un programa sobre la historia de España. Será útil para mis estudios.
2 (a) B (b) C

29. The cinema
1 Sample answers to follow-on questions:
   (a) Mi película favorita es *El señor de los anillos*. Me encanta el libro y creo que la película es una versión muy auténtica de la novela. Los paisajes son muy hermosos y los efectos especiales son increíbles. Cuenta una historia muy emocionante y los actores son excelentes.
   (b) No voy al cine mucho, porque es muy caro y se puede ver muchas películas en casa en Netflix y otros sitios. A veces, cuando hay una película que necesita una pantalla grande, entonces vale la pena ir al cine y lo paso bien.
2 Mi película favorita es la historia de una mujer que quiere ser una estrella. Es un musical, con unas canciones maravillosas, y ganó muchos premios. A veces es divertida, pero tiene algunos momentos tristes también. Voy a verla otra vez este fin de semana.

30. What's the story?
1 (a) comedy (b) action (c) girlfriend
2 Sample answer:
En la foto hay un hombre sentado en el salón de su casa. Es un salón bonito y moderno con paredes azules. El hombre está muy cómodo y está relajándose. Lleva una camisa y pantalones azules y zapatillas de deporte. Tiene el pelo negro. Está viendo un programa en la tele, que tiene una pantalla muy grande. El programa podría ser un documental sobre una ruta por las montañas. O podría ser una película en la que dos amigos van de vacaciones al campo en bicicleta y tienen muchas aventuras.
Sample responses to follow-on questions:
(a) Me encanta ir al cine porque la pantalla es muy grande y hay un ambiente especial. También el sonido es mejor.
(b) Fui con mis amigos el sábado pasado. Lo pasamos muy bien. Cuando era pequeño, iba con mis padres y mi hermana para ver películas familiares.

31. Celebrities and role models
1

Who …	Hugo	Alba	Emilio
(a) … is Peruvian?		×	
(b) … helps in a food bank?			×
(c) … is Cuban?	×		
(d) … helps victims of violence?		×	
(e) … is Bolivian?			×
(f) … helps the homeless?	×		

2 Sample answer:
Mi actriz favorita es Emma Watson. Tiene el pelo largo y marrón y los ojos marrones también. Es muy bonita. Creo que es un buen modelo de conducta para los jóvenes, especialmente para las chicas, porque dice cosas positivas sobre la igualdad de género. Leí un artículo sobre ella la semana pasada y descubrí que también ha sido modelo y que se interesa por el medio ambiente. Este fin de semana voy a ver una película en la que ella es la actriz principal.

32. Places in town
1 (a) market (b) port (c) on the corner
2 T: Sí. ¿Te puedo ayudar?
   S: Por favor, me gustaría ir a un supermercado.
   T: Te recomiendo ir a la calle mayor.
   S: ¿A qué hora abre?
   T: Todas las tiendas están abiertas ahora.
   S: ¿Cómo se llega?
   T: Está en esa calle a la derecha. ¿Algo más?
   S: También busco un sitio para comer.
   T: Ah, pues, ¿qué tipo de comida prefieres?
   S: Prefiero la comida española.
   T: Entonces, tienes que probar el restaurante al final de la calle.

33. Things to do in town
1 (a) B (b) A (c) C (d) A
2 (a) Irá de compras el martes.
   (b) Visitará el castillo este fin de semana.
   (c) Comeré / Cenaré en el café.
   (d) ¿Podrás jugar al fútbol el sábado?
   (e) Veré una película en la plaza.

34. Shopping for clothes
1

Who …	Sara	Luisa	Javier
(a) … likes being in fashion?		×	
(b) … never goes to the supermercado?	×		
(c) … occasionally shops online?			×
(d) … prefers the local shops?	×		
(e) … enjoys sales parties?		×	
(f) … tends to go to shopping centres?			×

2 T: Hola. ¿En qué puedo ayudarle?
   S: Quiero una camiseta.
   T: Muy bien. Están por aquí. ¿De qué talla?
   S: Quiero una camiseta pequeña.
   T: De acuerdo. Mire usted. ¿Qué color quiere?
   S: Quiero azul, por favor.
   T: Vale. ¿Es para una ocasión especial?
   S: Es para una fiesta de cumpleaños.
   T: Perfecto.
   S: ¿Cuánto es?
   T: Voy a buscar el precio.

35. Transport
1 To get to school previously I used to walk but now I go by bike because it's faster. If I want to go to the city, I usually catch the bus. It's not as comfortable as the train and it takes forty minutes but it's much cheaper. In the city / In town, you can catch the boat to cross to the island.
2 Sample answer:
En la foto vemos un tren con muchas personas. Las dos personas en el primer plano son una mujer y un hombre de negocios. Parece que los dos van al trabajo o a una reunión importante porque llevan traje y una camisa blanca, y el hombre tiene una corbata. Creo que es por la mañana porque los dos están tomando un café. La mujer está trabajando y está mirando

su portátil. El hombre está hablando en el móvil, probablemente molestando a las otras personas con su conversación en voz alta.
Sample answers to follow-on questions:
(a) No está mal. Hay muchos autobuses que van con frecuencia a la ciudad. No tenemos una estación de trenes en mi pueblo, pero es fácil coger el autobús y luego coger el tren en la ciudad.
(b) Cogí el tren para ir a la ciudad y usé la bicicleta bastante.

36. Travel on public transport and buying tickets

1 Sample answers:
 1 Hay un hombre en un traje gris.
 2 Está corriendo para coger el autobús.
 3 El autobús está saliendo.
 4 Creo que el hombre va a perder el autobús.
2 T: Hola. ¿En qué puedo ayudarle?
 S: Quiero ir a Barcelona.
 T: Y, ¿a qué hora?
 S: Prefiero ir a las tres de la tarde.
 T: De acuerdo. ¿Qué tipo de billetes quiere?
 S: Quiero dos billetes de ida y vuelta.
 T: Muy bien. ¿Por qué quiere ir?
 S: Voy a visitar a unos amigos.
 T: Perfecto. ¿Tiene una pregunta?
 S: ¿De dónde sale el autobús?
 T: Sale de aquí.

37. My region – good and bad

1 1 Hay unos **edificios hermosos** en la **ciudad**.
 2 El **paisaje** en las **montañas** es muy **tranquilo**.
 3 Seguimos el camino estrecho por el bosque.
 4 Construyeron la mezquita hace cuatro años.
 5 No permiten perros en esta zona.
 6 Me gustan los espacios verdes.
2 Sample answer:
Vivo en esta región desde pequeña.
Es una región bastante tranquila con mucho campo verde y pequeños pueblos. Por lo tanto, la gente piensa que es muy bonita y es popular con los turistas. La ciudad donde vivo tiene varios edificios históricos y un gran parque al lado del río. Sin embargo, no hay mucho para los jóvenes y a veces parece un poco aburrida. La semana pasada había un festival de comida en el parque y fui con mi madre para probar algunos productos típicos de la región. Pero también había puestos que vendían comida de otros países. Mi madre compró muchas cosas y lo pasamos bien. El fin de semana que viene, mis amigos y yo vamos a pasear en bicicleta por el campo y a hacer camping al lado del lago. Va a ser muy divertido.

38. My region in the past

1 Sample answers to follow-on questions:
(a) Aquí en mi pueblo no hay nada para los turistas, pero vivo cerca de dos ciudades importantes que atraen a muchos turistas. Hay restaurantes buenos, museos de arte, teatros y salas de conciertos. También, hay una zona de lagos, campo y montañas a una hora de aquí que es muy bonita.
(b) De momento estoy contento aquí, porque toda mi familia y mis amigos están en esta ciudad, pero en el futuro me gustaría vivir en otro país un rato.
2 (a) Hay muchos campos en mi región.
 (b) No tenemos espacios verdes en la ciudad.
 (c) Los vecinos en mi calle son muy simpáticos.
 (d) Me gusta el parque al lado del río.
 (e) Vivía en un pueblo pequeño.

39. Town or country?
1 (a) A C D (b) B E F
2 (a) B (b) C (c) B (d) B (e) A

40. Plans for the holidays
1 (a) getting up late (b) relaxing (c) in a shop (d) going on holiday (e) helping in the garden
2 (a) swimming pool (b) too many people (on a Saturday) (c) Monday (d) the pool is closed (for cleaning) (e) a bike ride (f) lunch / sandwiches and a drink

41. Holiday preferences
1 (a) Lola
Destination: United Kingdom
Reason: to practise English / to visit historic buildings
(b) David
Destination: Africa
Reason: very different landscapes / scenery / the people are/ seem nice
(c) Alba
Destination: Balearic Islands
Reason: lots for young people (to do) / the journey there is short / it doesn't take long to get there
2 T: ¿Adónde te gustaría ir más en el mundo? ¿Por qué?
 S: Me gustaría ir a América Latina. Creo que sería increíble visitar países como México y Argentina. Sería una experiencia maravillosa que nunca olvidaría.
 T: ¿Prefieres pasar las vacaciones en tu propio país o ir al extranjero?
 S: ¡Los dos! Lo ideal sería pasar una semana en junio en mi país, en el campo o en la costa. Después, me gustaría pasar una semana en España en octubre cuando todavía hace buen tiempo.
 T: ¿Qué destino prefieres para las vacaciones – la costa o las montañas?
 S: Prefiero la costa. Me encanta estar al lado del mar para tomar el sol en la playa. Normalmente hay muchas actividades que hacer también.
 T: ¿Qué piensas de pasar las vacaciones en una casa en el campo?
 S: Creo que sería muy aburrido. No hay mucho que hacer, y sería demasiado tranquilo.
 T: ¿Prefieres ir de vacaciones con tus amigos o con la familia? ¿Por qué?
 S: Siempre voy de vacaciones con mi familia y es muy divertido porque me llevo bien con mis hermanos y hacemos muchas actividades juntos. Pero un día me gustaría ir de vacaciones con mis amigos. Creo que lo pasaría muy bien.
 T: ¿En qué estación del año prefieres ir de vacaciones?
 S: Si voy de vacaciones en mi país, prefiero ir en verano porque hay más posibilidad de buen tiempo. Pero si voy al extranjero, a un país como España, a veces hace demasiado calor en verano y la primavera sería ideal.

42. Types of holidays
1

Who likes to …	Fátima	Luis	Pilar
(a) … go shopping?			×
(b) … be in the country?		×	
(c) … rent a car?	×		
(d) … eat out?			×
(e) … go sightseeing?	×		
(f) … get some exercise?		×	

2 Sample answer:
En la foto vemos a una familia que está de vacaciones. Están haciendo camping en un bosque y tienen tiendas de color azul y gris. El padre y el hijo mayor están sentados en sillas y también hay dos niñas. Todos están alrededor de un fuego. Están cocinando

algo. Creo que hace buen tiempo porque llevan camiseta y pantalones cortos.

Sample answers to follow-on questions:
(a) Me encantan. Me gusta mucho estar al lado del mar y tomar el sol en la playa. Nado en el mar y salgo a cenar con la familia por la tarde.
(b) Creo que pueden ser interesantes. Me gusta hacer una variedad de actividades cuando estoy de vacaciones. Es interesante visitar sitios históricos, pero también quiero ir a la playa.

43. Where to stay
1 (a) C (b) A (c) B (d) A (e) B (f) C
2 (a) Las instalaciones en el hotel son excelentes.
(b) Vamos a alojarnos / quedarnos / Nos vamos a alojar / Nos vamos a quedar en un camping de cinco estrellas.
(c) Espero alquilar una casa cerca de la playa.
(d) El piso estaba muy limpio y tenía una vista / vistas a la piscina.
(e) Llovió el jueves y fuimos a la sala de juegos.

44. Booking accommodation
1 T: Buenos días. ¿Cómo puedo ayudarle?
S: Quiero una habitación doble, por favor.
T: ¿Para cuántas noches?
S: Para tres noches.
T: ¿Qué vistas quiere?
S: Quiero una habitación con vistas al mar.
T: ¿Cuándo quiere comer?
S: Quiero comer a las dos.
T: Muy bien. ¿Algo más?
S: ¿A qué hora se abre el restaurante?
T: Se abre a las siete.
2 1 Las **vistas** son bastante **bonitas**.
   2 Quiero una **habitación** con **ducha**.
   3 Está **enfrente** de la **playa**.
   4 ¿Cuánto es el piso en total?
   5 Las piscinas están limpias.
   6 Los jardines eran pequeños.

45. Holiday activities
1 Sample answers:
   1 En la foto hay siete jóvenes.
   2 Están jugando al vóleibol en la playa.
   3 Hace muy buen tiempo.
   4 Los chicos están muy contentos.
2 Sample answers to follow-on questions:
(a) Me gusta tomar el sol en la playa y hacer natación en la piscina. También me gusta comer en restaurantes y hacer deporte al aire libre.
(b) Me gusta visitar castillos porque son interesantes, pero algunos edificios son un poco aburridos.

46. Trips and visits
1 T: Buenos días. ¿Cómo puedo ayudarle?
S: Me gustaría ir de excursión el viernes.
T: Vale. ¿A qué hora quiere ir?
S: Quiero ir a las diez.
T: Pues, hay varias. ¿Qué tipo de excursión busca?
S: Tengo ganas de hacer una excursión en barco.
T: Aquí hay una que sería ideal.
S: ¿Cuánto cuestan los billetes?
T: Son ocho euros por persona.
S: ¿A qué hora volveremos?
T: Volvemos bastante tarde.

2 Several days ago, we went on a trip to the mountains (to the) north of the city / town. We went by bus / coach and the journey took an hour and a half. We stopped in a village to eat / for lunch and there was snow everywhere. Today we are buying / shopping for souvenirs at the market, but tomorrow I am very keen to visit the castle.

47. Giving or asking for directions
1 T: ¿Sí? ¿Cómo puedo ayudarle?
S: Por favor, ¿a qué hora abre el supermercado?
T: A las nueve. ¿Cuál es su nacionalidad?
S: Soy inglés.
T: Muy bien. ¿Qué piensa de la ciudad?
S: Me gusta mucho, es muy bonita.
T: ¿Y dónde se aloja usted?
S: Estamos en el hotel Miramar.
T: Muy bien. ¿Cuándo vuelve a casa?
S: Vuelvo a casa mañana.
T: De acuerdo.
2 (a) follow the street on the right (b) cross the bridge
  (c) take the street to the left (d) 50 metres
  (e) a park (f) at 7 o'clock

48. Shopping for gifts
1 Sample answer:
Hay dos personas en la foto, un chico y una chica. Creo que son hermanos porque se parecen mucho. Son jóvenes y tienen el pelo rubio. La chica lleva un vestido verde y el chico tiene una camiseta amarilla. Están en una tienda de ropa y están mirando una camisa azul. Están pensando en comprarla, probablemente para el chico o para su padre. También tienen varias bolsas de muchos colores porque han comprado cosas en otras tiendas.

Sample answers to follow-on questions:
(a) Mis amigos y yo no compramos regalos, pero compro regalos de cumpleaños para mi madre. A menudo compro flores o chocolates.
(b) Fuimos a la ciudad para ir de compras porque hay una gran variedad de tiendas allí. Compré ropa para una fiesta que hay al final del mes. Compré zapatillas de deporte también.
2 (a) B (b) A (c) B (d) C

49. Tourist information
1 1 El **puente romano** es muy **hermoso**.
   2 No se permiten **motocicletas** en el **casco urbano**.
   3 El turismo es esencial aquí.
   4 Van a cerrar la oficina pronto.
   5 Cogimos un horario en la biblioteca.
   6 Tengo ganas de ver el edificio nuevo.
2 (a) Voy a la oficina de turismo.
  (b) Queremos una lista de hoteles en la zona / región.
  (c) El mapa / El plano enseña / muestra muchos sitios interesantes.
  (d) Ayer mi hermano y yo alquilamos bicicletas.
  (e) El castillo no está abierto al público.

50. Tourist attractions
1 We have just spent the day in Barcelona. Without a doubt, it is a beautiful city with lots of places of interest. I enjoyed walking along the big street from the square to the port, with the flower stalls and numerous cafés. It is worth going to see the park and the buildings. The architecture is very interesting.
2 Sample answer:
Mientras estás aquí vale la pena ir a la ciudad para ver el puerto y los museos en esa zona. Es una zona bonita con muchos edificios interesantes.

También tienes que pasar tiempo en el campo porque hay unos caminos bonitos al lado del río y en el valle.

La semana pasada fui a un concierto en el estadio en la ciudad. Muchas bandas y muchos cantantes actúan allí.

Durante tu visita, ¿por qué no vamos al campo juntos? Podríamos ir en bicicleta y llevar una merienda.

51. Holiday problems
1 A, C, D
2 Sample answers:

Me gusta hacer viajes diferentes en vacaciones. Es maravilloso estar en la playa cuando hace sol y puedes entrar al mar. Pero también me encanta hacer turismo y ver todos los sitios de interés en la zona.

Cuando vas de vacaciones en este país, siempre hay el riesgo de tener mal tiempo porque la lluvia afecta muchas de las actividades que quieres hacer. Sin embargo, hay mucho que hacer y numerosas regiones hermosas.

El año pasado fuimos al norte de España en barco y, durante el viaje, mi madre perdió su pasaporte. Tuvimos que ir a la policía cuando llegamos para resolver el problema.

Un día me gustaría visitar México. Quiero probar la comida y experimentar las fiestas y costumbres de ese país. La cultura mexicana es muy interesante, y me encantaría estar allí para ver los desfiles del Día de los Muertos.

52. Accommodation problems
1 (a) his wife (b) near the café (c) young people are making a noise (d) silence after 10.30
   (e) The receptionist should talk to the young people.
   (f) move Nicolás to another part of the campsite
2 (a) Hay un problema con la cuenta.
   (b) Los cuchillos en el piso están sucios.
   (c) ¿Tiene(s) una habitación doble?
   (d) Pedimos una habitación con vistas / vista al mar.
   (e) No estoy contento/a con la habitación.

53. Eating out
1 T: Buenos días. ¿Cómo puedo ayudarle?
   S: Quiero una mesa al lado de la ventana.
   T: Muy bien. ¿Qué quiere tomar?
   S: Quisiera una tortilla de queso con patatas fritas.
   T: ¿Y para beber?
   S: Una botella de agua.
   T: ¿Está todo bien?
   S: Sí, me gusta mucho.
   T: Muy bien. ¿Algo más?
   S: ¿Cuánto es, por favor?
   T: 10 euros.
2 (a) a table for two (b) by the window
   (c) if the pasta is made with meat / if there is meat in the pasta dish
   (d) it is made with vegetables / it is a vegetarian dish
   (e) fish and rice
   (f) (a bottle of) water

54. Opinions about food
1 Sample answer:
En la foto hay un grupo de amigos, tres mujeres y dos hombres. La mujer en el centro lleva gafas y un sombrero. Están en un café y creo que el café está en un centro comercial. Están tomando hamburguesas y patatas fritas. Se ven muy contentos.
Sample responses to follow-on questions:
(a) Prefiero comida sana como el pescado, la pasta y las verduras. No me gustan mucho los postres ni el chocolate pero como bastante fruta.

(b) Creo que la comida rápida no es muy sana, pero de vez en cuando me gusta tomar una hamburguesa con patatas fritas.
2 1 La **paella** está muy **rica**.
   2 Soy **alérgico** a los **mariscos**.
   3 Aquí **hacen** churros **fantásticos**.
   4 Prefiero la comida con carne.
   5 Los postres son demasiado caros.
   6 Quiero tomar la tortilla.

55. The weather
1 Sample answers:
   1 Hay cuatro personas en la foto.
   2 Una madre juega con sus tres hijos.
   3 Está nevando y están haciendo un hombre de nieve.
   4 Llevan jerseys y chaquetas porque hace mucho frío.
2 (a) It is cold today and I think it is going to snow.
   (b) There is a chance / the risk of very high temperatures.
   (c) Tomorrow it will be hot and sunny all day.
   (d) It was very windy on the coast yesterday.
   (e) It is raining and there are lots of grey clouds in the sky.

56. Customs and festivals
1 (a) books and roses / The man gives roses and the woman gives a book.
   (b) They are filled with stalls selling books.
   (c) The book sellers arrive to set up their stalls.
   (d) An author comes and signs copies of their book.
   (e) It was when the fiesta / festival started.
   (f) To commemorate the deaths of Cervantes and Shakespeare.
2 A, B, D

57. A visit to Barcelona
1 (a) B (b) A (c) C
2 B, C, E

58. A visit to Buenos Aires
1 (a) A (b) B (c) B (d) C
2 Sample answer:
En la foto se puede ver una calle y un café al aire libre. En primer plano hay un hombre y una mujer que están bailando en la calle. Creo que podría ser una foto de Buenos Aires porque parece que están bailando tango. Nadie está mirando a la pareja que baila; una mujer con un sombrero lleva una caja grande y azul por la calle, dos perros están dormidos y la gente en el café come, bebe y habla.

Sample answers to follow-on questions:
(a) A mí no me interesan mucho porque no entiendo nada de bailar, pero los programas son muy populares y muchas personas los ven cada semana.
(b) Visité la ciudad de Bath con mi clase de historia del instituto. Es una ciudad muy histórica y bonita con muchos monumentos antiguos y edificios famosos. Lo pasé muy bien.

59. School subjects
1 (a) A (b) C (c) B
2 Sample answers to follow-on questions:
(a) Estudio inglés, matemáticas, ciencias, español, historia y dibujo.
(b) Me parecen muy difíciles. No saco buenas notas y creo que no voy a aprobar el examen en verano.

60. School subjects – likes and dislikes
1 1 Normalmente **saca** buenas **notas** en **francés**.
   2 No tengo **talento** en **dibujo** pero es **fascinante**.
   3 Me gusta la ciencia.
   4 La tecnología es aburrida a veces.
   5 La historia es una asignatura muy útil.
   6 Mi clase favorita es la educación física.

2 Sample answer:
En este momento estudio inglés, matemáticas, ciencias, historia, tecnología, educación física y religión. Tengo mucha suerte porque me gustan todas mis asignaturas.
Me encanta el español porque las clases son divertidas y me gusta practicar el idioma cuando voy de vacaciones a España.
Dejé el dibujo en el tercer curso porque es difícil para mí y no sacaba buenas notas.
El año próximo voy a continuar con el español, el inglés y una asignatura más. No sé cuál voy a escoger. Voy a ver mis notas después de los exámenes antes de decidir.

61. The school day

1

Who …	Andrea	Iván	Dani
(a) … has a long lunch hour?		×	
(b) … can't walk to school?	×		
(c) … has a snack at break?			×
(d) … wants better facilities outside?			×
(e) … can't join in the school clubs?	×		
(f) … wants to shorten the school day?		×	

2 Sample answer:
En mi instituto, la primera clase empieza a las ocho y media y terminamos a las tres y veinticinco.
Después de las clases hay una gran variedad de clubs y actividades que son muy interesantes. Hay un club de teatro, muchas actividades deportivas y varios clubs musicales.
Ayer decidí ir al colegio a pie porque hacía sol. Normalmente voy en coche con mi padre, pero ayer fui andando; me reuní con mi amigo y caminamos juntos.
Mañana iré en coche porque tengo que llevar mi equipo de deporte. Hay educación física primero, y luego matemáticas, historia y ciencias.

62. School facilities
1 (a) Karima
 Advantage: modern gym
 Disadvantage: not enough computers (in technology)
 (b) Daniel
 Advantage: excellent library
 Disadvantage: playground / yard is too small
 (c) Leya
 Advantage: opportunity to do an exchange abroad
 Disadvantage: no after-school clubs
2 Sample answer:
 1 Hay cuatro jóvenes en la biblioteca del instituto.
 2 Están estudiando y usando varios recursos.
 3 Están utilizando bolígrafos para escribir en sus cuadernos.
 4 También están buscando información en Internet en el portátil.

63. School uniform

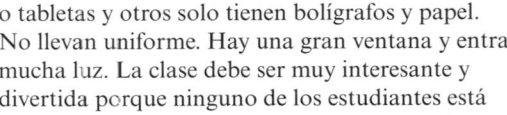

1 Sample answer:
En la foto podemos ver a un grupo de nueve estudiantes con su profesora en una clase de música. Los estudiantes llevan uniforme: una chaqueta azul y una camisa azul. Los chicos también llevan corbata. Están cantando una canción y parecen contentos. En la clase hay varias pantallas.
Sample answers to follow-on questions:
(a) No está mal, llevamos una chaqueta roja oscura y una falda o pantalones grises. Los zapatos y calcetines tienen que ser negros. No llevamos jersey, pero la corbata es blanca y negra.
(b) Me gustaría cambiar la camisa, que es azul. Prefiero tener una camisa blanca con los colores del resto del uniforme.
2 (a) C (b) B (c) A

64. Activities in class

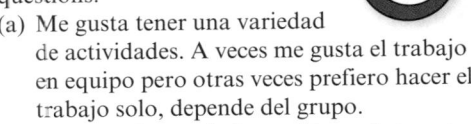

1 Sample answers to follow-on questions:
(a) Me gusta tener una variedad de actividades. A veces me gusta el trabajo en equipo pero otras veces prefiero hacer el trabajo solo, depende del grupo.
(b) Me gusta buscar información en Internet y hacer ejercicios en línea. Algunos de los juegos educativos son bastante divertidos. Pero tienes que escribir y leer también; es una parte importante de estudiar.
2 Sample answer:
En mi instituto tenemos cuatro clases por la mañana y dos por la tarde. Hay un descanso después de la segunda clase.
Me gustan más las clases de español porque hacemos una gran variedad de actividades y nunca son aburridas.
Por ejemplo, la semana pasada, hablamos de las vacaciones y aprendimos nuevas palabras. También, hicimos ejercicios de escuchar y leer usando los ordenadores.
La semana próxima, en la clase de religión vamos a tener un debate. Antes de la clase tenemos que buscar información y preparar nuestras ideas y opiniones.

65. School rules
1 1 Las **normas** son **justas**.
 2 No **podemos** comer **chicle**.
 3 Tenemos que **llevar** el uniforme **correcto**.
 4 Hay que escuchar bien.
 5 Debemos hacer los deberes.
 6 Está prohibido correr en el colegio.
2 (a) Tienes que / Debes / Hay que hacer los deberes todos los días / cada día.
 (b) Nunca llegamos tarde al instituto / colegio.
 (c) No debes / No hay que / No se debe tirar basura en el patio.
 (d) No puedes traer / llevar el móvil a (la) clase.
 (e) Siempre debemos tener el equipo necesario.

66. School – the good and the bad
1 (a) The place she likes: the library
 The reason she likes it: it has lots of new computers
 (b) The problem she mentions: (lack of) equality
 The example she gives: no girls' football team
2 (a) El director es muy estricto. / La directora es muy estricta.
 (b) Aprobé el examen la semana pasada.
 (c) Podemos hacer preguntas en clase.
 (d) Algo que me gusta mucho es el uso de la tecnología.
 (e) Algunos profesores nos dan demasiados deberes. / Algunas profesoras nos dan demasiados deberes.

67. School clubs and activities
1 (a) C (b) B (c) C (d) A (e) B (f) A
2 (a) when she went on an exchange to England / with an English girl
 (b) after school / after classes
 (c) two of: dance classes, English lessons, learning to play an instrument
 (d) you have to pay; the schools that organise them are private

68. Being a good student
1 A, C, F
2 Sample answer:
En la foto hay una clase de estudiantes, chicos y chicas, y su profesor. Algunos tienen portátiles o tabletas y otros solo tienen bolígrafos y papel. No llevan uniforme. Hay una gran ventana y entra mucha luz. La clase debe ser muy interesante y divertida porque ninguno de los estudiantes está aburrido. Todos parecen felices y algunos quieren participar. Creo que el profesor acaba de hacer una pregunta. Algunos de los estudiantes quieren contestar.

Sample answers to follow-on questions:
(a) Llevo el material correcto a la clase, siempre escucho al profesor y nunca hablo cuando el profesor está hablando. Hago mis deberes con tiempo y nunca los entrego sin terminar.
(b) Leí y escribí mucho, practiqué con ejemplos de exámenes anteriores y mi madre me ayudó, haciéndome preguntas que tuve que contestar sin mirar el libro de texto.

69. Options at 16
1 (a) C (b) A (c) C (d) B
2 Sample answers to follow-on questions:
(a) Mis asignaturas favoritas son el inglés, la historia y el dibujo. Son interesantes y bastante fáciles. Saco buenas notas en estas asignaturas y los profesores son excelentes.
(b) Creo que no voy a continuar con las asignaturas tradicionales. Estoy pensando en ir a otro colegio para hacer un curso de formación profesional, posiblemente en turismo.

70. Equality
1

	Who talks about …	Malek	Carmen	Ana
(a)	… discrimination in school?		×	
(b)	… religious discrimination?			×
(c)	… pay inequality?	×		
(d)	… racial discrimination?		×	
(e)	… gender discrimination?	×		
(f)	… discrimination because of clothing?			×

2 Nuestro/a nuevo/a director/a ha mejorado muchas de las instalaciones del instituto para crear una mejor experiencia para las personas con discapacidad. Ahora tenemos un ascensor para llevar / subir las sillas de ruedas al primer piso. Si, por alguna razón, no pueden asistir a clase, pueden participar desde (su) casa en el portátil.

71. Future study plans
1 (a) Natalia
likes: the vocational / professional training courses
dislikes: that it / the college is far from home
(b) Juan
likes: the technology resources
dislikes: the sports facilities
2 T: ¿Qué planes tienes para tus estudios el año próximo?
S: Tengo la intención de ir a un colegio local para estudiar matemáticas, ciencias y español.
T: ¿Cuáles son tus razones para escoger este curso?
S: Se me dan bien las ciencias en el instituto y es mejor estudiar matemáticas también porque las dos asignaturas van bien juntas. Quiero estudiar español simplemente porque me gusta, y será una clase muy diferente de las otras.
T: ¿Quieres ir a la universidad?
S: Sí, tengo muchas ganas de ir a la universidad porque he decidido que quiero ser médica en el futuro. Entonces, me hace falta estudiar medicina y sacar un título.
T: ¿Cuáles son los beneficios de ir a la universidad?
S: Creo que puedes conseguir un trabajo mejor pagado si tienes un título universitario y tienes más opciones de trabajo en general. También, hay muchas actividades sociales y oportunidades interesantes además de los estudios.
T: ¿Cuáles son los aspectos negativos?
S: Son más años de estudio sin ganar un salario, y esto puede ser duro. Sé que muchos estudiantes trabajan al mismo tiempo que estudian, pero esto crea mucha presión.

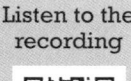

T: ¿Qué otras cosas te gustaría aprender en el futuro?
S: Hay muchas cosas que me gustaría aprender. Quiero aprender a hacer mi propia ropa y quiero aprender otro idioma, como el francés. El año próximo, voy a aprender a conducir*.

conducir (to drive) is not on the prescribed list but you can use words not from the list, as long as they are correct.

72. Future plans
1 1 Voy a **abrir** una **cuenta bancaria**.
   2 Me gustaría **mudarme** a otra **comunidad autónoma**.
   3 Mi sueño es viajar por el mundo.
   4 Quiero hacer una carrera universitaria.
   5 Mi objetivo es tener mucho éxito.
   6 Cuando sea mayor, tendré más independencia.
2 Sample answer:
En este momento estudio ocho asignaturas diferentes y mis favoritas son la educación física, el inglés y la historia. Mis estudios van bien y saco buenas notas en las pruebas, aunque no en matemáticas porque no las comprendo.
Espero ir a la universidad cuando tenga dieciocho años. Lo bueno de ir a la universidad es estudiar tu asignatura preferida por tres o cuatro años y salir al final con un título. Lo difícil sería pasar más años sin salario.
Cuando era pequeño, quería ser médico. Veía programas sobre los hospitales y cómo los doctores salvaban la vida de otras personas, pero no sabía que para ser médico tienes que ser muy bueno en ciencias.
El septiembre próximo continuaré con mis tres asignaturas favoritas y creo que iré a la universidad para estudiar ciencias del deporte. Pienso que me gustaría ser profesor de educación física en una escuela primaria.

73. Part-time jobs and money
1 (a) Sundays (b) checkout / on the tills (c) 8 o'clock
2 Sample answers:
   1 Hay una chica joven que trabaja en un café.
   2 El hombre está comprando un café y un pastel.
   3 El hombre lleva una camisa azul.
   4 Está pagando con tarjeta.

74. Opinions about jobs
1

	Who asks about …	Pilar	Andrea	Marcos
(a)	… being a writer?			×
(b)	… choosing a subject?			×
(c)	… joining the police?		×	
(d)	… becoming a teacher?	×		
(e)	… doing training?	×		
(f)	… the money you earn?			×

2 Sample answers for follow-on questions:
(a) Trabajar con otras personas y tener compañeros simpáticos. También es importante llevarte bien con el jefe o la jefa.
(b) En este momento no tengo la menor idea, pero tengo que decidir pronto porque quiero ir a la universidad. Allí tendré tiempo para aprender más sobre las carreras que existen y las opciones que hay.

75. Pros and cons of different jobs
1 Sample answer:
En la foto podemos ver una oficina moderna con una gran ventana para dejar entrar la luz y una escalera que va a la puerta principal. Hay seis personas en la foto y creo que son las nueve de la mañana porque tres de las personas acaban de llegar al

149

trabajo. Un hombre ha venido en bicicleta y va a guardar la bici en la oficina para mantenerla segura. Dos personas están bajando la escalera y dos mujeres ya han empezado a trabajar. Un hombre está sentado en otra mesa trabajando con su ordenador.
Sample answers to follow-on questions:
(a) No me importa trabajar en una oficina, pero el trabajo tiene que ser interesante. Si estoy haciendo algo que me gusta, entonces el lugar no es importante. Otro aspecto esencial es tener compañeros simpáticos.
(b) El fin de semana pasado lavé el coche de mis padres y me dieron dinero. También cuidé a los niños de la vecina el viernes por la noche.
2 (a) I want to work in an office with modern equipment.
   (b) There are lots of rules in this company / firm.
   (c) Paula hopes / wants to be a scientist or a teacher.
   (d) I went abroad six times when I worked for the company.
   (e) I would not like to be a doctor, it's too much responsibility.

76. Job adverts, skills needed
1 (a) Necesito llamar a la empresa / compañía.
   (b) Soy trabajador/a y tengo una actitud positiva.
   (c) Busco / Estoy buscando información en línea.
   (d) Mi hermana encontró un trabajo en el periódico.
   (e) La empresa / compañía quiere gente con experiencia.
2 T: ¿Por qué eres la persona ideal para el trabajo?
   S: Soy trabajador y me llevo bien con la gente.
   T: Y ¿por qué quieres el trabajo?
   S: Quiero practicar el español y ganar experiencia.
   T: ¿Cuándo puedes empezar?
   S: Puedo empezar al principio de julio.
   T: Perfecto. ¿Tienes alguna pregunta?
   S: ¿Cómo será mi horario?
   T: De las nueve a las cinco. ¿Algo más?
   S: ¿Cuánto dinero voy a ganar?
   T: Son quince euros por hora.

77. Applying for jobs
1 (a) B (b) C (c) C
2 1 Voy a **llamar** a este **número**.
   2 Mi **entrevista** es **mañana**.
   3 Tus **compañeros** parecen muy **simpáticos**.
   4 La empresa está cerca.
   5 Tengo que mandar una carta.
   6 He trabajado en un restaurante.

78. Preparing for interviews
1 Sample answer:
En la foto hay cinco personas sentadas en fila. Creo que están esperando una entrevista. Los tres hombres llevan pantalón y chaqueta. Todos están muy serios y probablemente están nerviosos. Uno de los hombres está mirando la hora porque quiere saber cuánto tiempo queda antes de su entrevista. Todas las personas están mirando información, en papeles o en el móvil. Podrían estar pensando en ideas sobre lo que van a decir en la entrevista o mirando una presentación que tienen que dar.
Sample answers to follow-on questions:
(a) Me gustaría trabajar en un hotel o restaurante en Murcia. Podría practicar el español hablando con los clientes y ganar dinero al mismo tiempo. Durante mis días libres, iría a la playa.
(b) Fui a una entrevista de trabajo y llevé una falda negra, una camisa blanca y una chaqueta verde.
2 Yesterday I went to the Tourist Office for an interview. I wore a grey suit, a white shirt and a red tie. I felt quite nervous, but the boss was very nice / friendly and when he asked me questions, I could answer with confidence. At the end, he told me that they would call me this Thursday to tell me if I have been successful.

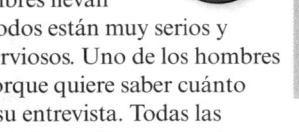

79. Working to help others
1 (a) reads (stories) to children
   (b) looks after her neighbour's garden / gardening for her neighbour
   (c) home for elderly
2 Sample answers:
   1 Hay un profesor trabajando en una escuela.
   2 Está en una clase con niños pequeños.
   3 Está ayudando a los niños con sus dibujos.
   4 Lleva una camiseta azul y está contento.

80. Equality and helping others
1 A, B, E
2 Sample answer:
En la foto hay dos hombres que acaban de terminar un partido de tenis. Están en sillas de ruedas y llevan pantalón corto y una camiseta en blanco y negro. Están en un gran estadio y debe ser una competición importante porque hay muchas personas allí viendo el partido. No sabemos quién ganó el partido – es difícil descubrirlo en sus expresiones.
Sample answers to follow-on questions:
(a) Creo que sí. Todos tenemos las mismas oportunidades para estudiar las asignaturas que queremos. Tenemos un ascensor y puertas amplias para las sillas de ruedas. Creo que el uniforme es un poco sexista porque los chicos no pueden llevar falda.
(b) Hace un año un amigo estaba enfermo y no podía ir al instituto. Fui a visitarlo varias veces, expliqué el trabajo que hacíamos en clase y le llevé los deberes. Le presté mi portátil para usarlo mientras se recuperaba.

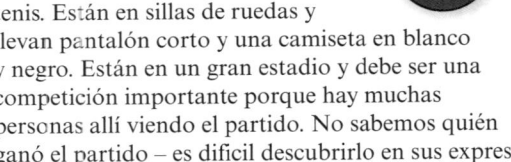

81. The environment and me
1 Sample answer:
Voy al instituto a pie porque no está muy lejos de mi casa. Llego al colegio en unos veinte minutos.
El transporte público en mi región no es muy bueno. No tenemos estación de trenes y no hay muchos autobuses.
La semana pasada, apagué todos los ordenadores al final de la clase de tecnología y ayudé con el reciclaje de botellas de plástico.
En el futuro, voy a ponerme más ropa y a bajar la temperatura en casa para usar menos energía.
2 Es muy importante proteger el planeta y hacer lo que podamos para cuidar el medio ambiente. En nuestra casa, solemos reciclar el papel, las botellas y el plástico. Cuando salí la semana pasada, usé el transporte público. Mi hermana va a llevar su ropa usada a una tienda de segunda mano.

82. Local environmental issues
1 Sample answer:
La foto es de un grupo de ocho jóvenes trabajando en equipo para limpiar el parque en su barrio. Todos los miembros del equipo llevan una camiseta azul y están recogiendo la basura que la gente ha tirado. El parque parece estar en una ciudad y debe ser un sitio que muchas personas visitan. Creo que están haciendo un trabajo muy importante para cuidar el medio ambiente y mantener limpios los espacios verdes.
Sample answers to follow-up questions:
(a) Lo peor de mi pueblo es la cantidad de basura. La gente tira papel, botellas y bolsas de plástico en las calles y no les importa nada. Hay un grupo de personas que recoge la basura de vez en cuando, pero en mi opinión, no debería de ser necesario.
(b) Cerca de mi casa hay un pequeño río y estaba lleno de basura. Yo pasé un fin de semana ayudando a limpiarlo para dar a los peces y a los pájaros una zona más limpia donde vivir.
2 (a) Hay mucha polución en el mar.
   (b) Me gustan los espacios verdes en la ciudad.
   (c) Vamos a caminar a la ciudad.

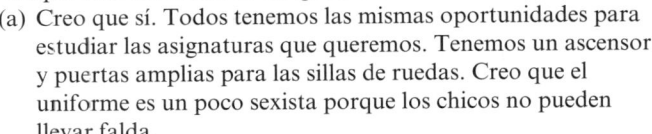

(d) Mi madre odiaba el ruido de la carretera.
(e) El aire está más limpio en el campo.

83. Global environmental issues
1 (a) B (b) C (c) A
2 1 **Debemos** usar menos **envases** para la **comida**.
   2 Siguen **talando** muchos **árboles** en la **selva**.
   3 Parte del bosque fue quemado.
   4 Las inundaciones siempre son graves.
   5 En algunas zonas hay falta de agua.
   6 No saben cuándo vendrán las lluvias.

84. Caring for the planet
1

Who …	Andrea	Carla	Raúl
(a) … is grateful to a band of volunteers?			×
(b) … feels that world leaders are not doing enough?		×	
(c) … is taking part in a protest march?	×		
(d) … has seen nature return to a once-polluted area?			×
(e) … is concerned about breathing contaminated air?	×		
(f) … believes the changing climate is a threat to life?		×	

2 (a) Lo primero es parar el cambio climático. Los gobiernos tienen que hacer mucho más para bajar las temperaturas y reducir el uso de la energía en los países del mundo.
   (b) Yo vivo en la costa y están intentando mantener las playas limpias. Esto es importante para la salud de los peces y pájaros que viven en estas zonas.

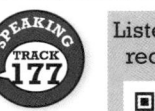

85. A greener future
1 Sample answer:
En la foto puedo ver un grupo de niños con sus profesores. Están en el parque cerca de su escuela para estudiar la naturaleza. Están aprendiendo sobre las flores y los árboles. Es una competición y tienen que responder a unas preguntas en un papel. Creo que está muy bien estudiar el medio ambiente cuando eres joven.
Sample answers to follow-on questions:
(a) Me gusta pasear al lado de un río o del mar. Me gusta mucho estar cerca del agua y ver los peces y los pájaros. Es muy relajante.
(b) Sí, me parece muy importante. Debemos aprender los efectos negativos que causamos en el planeta y encontrar maneras de resolverlos en el futuro.
2 Creo que el gobierno debería gastar más en el desarrollo de los recursos renovables. El sol, el viento y el mar tienen mucho poder y podremos usarlos para crear energía. Además, es energía limpia que causa menos polución. Leí esta información en línea.

86. Practice for Paper 1: Speaking
1 Sample answers to follow-on questions:
(a) Mi ciudad es grande con muchas tiendas, restaurantes y oficinas. Hay un gran centro comercial y un cine moderno. El transporte es bueno, pero también hay muchos coches.

(b) En mi opinión, el peor problema es la polución del mar cerca de donde vivo. La gente deja botellas de plástico en la playa.
2 Sample answers to follow-on questions:
(a) Soy una persona alegre y positiva y mis amigos me dicen que soy simpático. Me gusta mucho pasarlo bien y divertirme. Mis profesores piensan que debería ser un poco más serio y trabajador.
(b) Creo que sí, porque tus padres te dan toda su atención y no tienes que compartir nada con hermanos. Por otra parte, si tienes hermanos siempre puedes hablar con ellos y hacer actividades juntos.

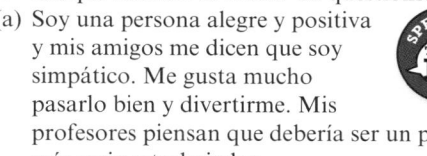

87. Practice for Paper 1: Speaking
1 T: Hola. ¿Cómo puedo ayudarle?
   S: ¿Cuánto cuesta entrar en la piscina?
   T: Depende. ¿Para quién es?
   S: Es para mi familia y para mí.
   T: Son cinco euros por persona. ¿Qué otros deportes le interesan?
   S: Me gusta el tenis y el baloncesto.
   T: Muy bien. ¿Dónde se aloja usted?
   S: Estamos en el camping cerca de aquí.
   T: ¿Tiene otra pregunta?
   S: ¿Cuándo está abierta la piscina?
   T: De las siete a las nueve cada día.
2 Sample answer:
Es una foto de una playa en verano. Hay mucha gente allí tomando el sol y bañándose en el mar. El cielo es azul sin nubes y la arena está muy limpia. El mar está tranquilo y creo que hace mucho calor. A lo lejos se puede ver edificios altos, probablemente hoteles y pisos. Hay un ambiente alegre porque la gente está de vacaciones, hace buen tiempo y están contentos.
Sample answers to follow-on questions:
(a) No me interesan mucho, parecen bastante aburridas porque no haces nada salvo tomar el sol. A mí me gustan más las vacaciones más activas, probando varias actividades nuevas y pasando el tiempo con amigos.
(b) El verano pasado pasé un fin de semana en un centro de actividades en el campo. Había un río y un gran bosque con muchos caminos para andar o pasear en bici. Había un montón de actividades para probar, como montar a caballo, natación y tenis. Lo pasé muy bien.

88. Practice for Paper 2: Listening
1 (a) B (b) A
2 C, E, F
3 (a) square (b) port (c) 15th

89. Practice for Paper 2: Listening
1 (a) Sofia
   likes: (classes with) group activities
   dislikes: difficult Maths exercises
   (b) Nadim
   likes: finishing at 2.30 / classes ending early
   dislikes: the expensive uniform / the cost of the uniform
2 1 Faltan **rampas** para las **sillas** de **ruedas**.
   2 Hay que **instalar** un **ascensor** cerca de la **escalera**.
   3 Queremos más mujeres en el gobierno.
   4 La actriz pide igual salario.
   5 Mis compañeros se manifestaron en la calle.
   6 Es una empresa multicultural sin discriminación.

90. Practice for Paper 3: Reading

1

Who …	Carla	Daniel	Monika
(a) … thought the starters were great?			×
(b) … was there for a family event?	×		
(c) … found the desserts disappointing?			×
(d) … enjoyed all the food?	×		
(e) … thought the price was reasonable?		×	
(f) … was served a cold drink?		×	

2 (a) A (b) C (c) B

91. Practice for Paper 3: Reading

1 (a) Job A
One thing you will learn: to look after horses / to feed the horses
Your afternoon task: help with horse riding classes
(b) Job B
Your main job: making cheese and yoghurt
Your other task: working in the shops / selling the products I made
(c) Job C
Your role in the mornings: explaining the farm work to visitors
Your role during the trip: explaining the region's history
(d) B

2 I am the boss / manager of a group of people who work with me in the sales office of a large company / firm. Yesterday there was a meeting with the other bosses / managers and, several times, one of them started to talk when I was talking. He thinks that his opinion is more important than mine. It makes me very cross. / It really annoys me.

92. Practice for Paper 4: Writing

1 Sample answers:
  1 Hay un chico en un cuarto de su casa.
  2 Está haciendo sus deberes.
  3 Tiene un portátil y algunos libros.
  4 Piensa que los deberes son difíciles.

2 Sample answer:
Cuando voy de compras me gusta comprar ropa y zapatos. Me gustan las camisetas y las zapatillas de deporte. Las tiendas en mi pueblo son pequeñas y caras. Voy a la ciudad para comprar la ropa porque hay más opciones. Voy a ir de compras al centro comercial este sábado.

3 (a) Hay muchos coches en la ciudad.
  (b) El aeropuerto no está muy lejos.
  (c) Queremos alquilar bicicletas esta tarde.
  (d) Tengo mi pasaporte y nuestros billetes.
  (e) Fui a la isla en barco ayer.

93. Practice for Paper 4: Writing

1 Sample answer:
Un buen amigo es una persona que siempre está ahí cuando lo necesitas y está listo para ayudar y apoyarte cuando tienes un problema. Un buen amigo te escucha y te entiende. También comparte algunos de tus intereses y tiene el mismo sentido del humor. Así, puede hacerte reír si estás triste.
Mi mejor amigo, Mike, es muy simpático y divertido y lo pasamos bien juntos. Pero no estudia mucho y mis padres piensan que es una mala influencia.
Cuando Mike tenía problemas para aprender los detalles para el examen de historia, yo le ayudé a aprenderlos. Pasé varias tardes en su casa estudiando con él.
Durante las vacaciones de verano, voy a coger el tren para ir a la costa con un grupo de amigos. Nos bañaremos en el mar y jugaremos al vóleibol en la playa.

2 Para tener / llevar una vida sana, es importante hacer ejercicio y comer una variedad de comidas diferentes. Sin embargo, también necesitas descansar y dormir bien. Tener pasatiempos es una buena manera de relajarte. Ayer leí una revista y jugué al tenis. Mi hermano ganó el partido.

94. Nouns and articles

1 (a) la (b) el (c) las (d) los (e) la (f) el (g) las (h) los (i) el (j) la
2 (a) las (b) un (c) el (d) los (e) una (f) un (g) el (h) El
3 (b) Mi padre es ~~un~~ policía y mi madre es ~~una~~ médica.
  (c) Hay muy pocos estudiantes en el instituto sin ~~un~~ móvil.
  (d) Escribo con ~~un~~ bolígrafo en mi clase de matemáticas.
  (e) En el futuro me gustaría ser ~~una~~ actriz.
  (h) Se puede reservar dos habitaciones con ~~una~~ ducha.

95. Adjectives

1 (a) cómoda (b) contentos (c) rojo (d) interesantes
  (e) español (f) simpáticas (g) bonita (h) baratos
2 (a) moderno (b) cómodos (c) bueno (d) importante
  (e) limpia (f) útiles
3 (a) En Inglaterra hay **poca** gente que habla muy bien castellano.
  (b) Lo mejor es que tiene un jardín **bonito**.
  (c) Estamos **contentas** porque hace buen tiempo.
  (d) En el futuro habrá una **gran** estación en las afueras de la ciudad.
  (e) Mi abuela vive en el **primer** piso.

96. Possessives and pronouns

1

English	Spanish singular	Spanish plural
my	mi	**mis**
your	**tu**	tus
his / her / its	**su**	**sus**
our	**nuestro / nuestra**	nuestros / nuestras
your	**vuestro / vuestra**	**vuestros / vuestras**
their	su	sus

2 (a) Mi (b) Su (c) Sus (d) Mis (e) Su
3 (a) el mío (b) las suyas (c) el nuestro (d) el tuyo
4 (a) María tiene un gato que es negro y pequeño.
  (b) Vivimos en un pueblo que está en el norte de Ecuador.
  (c) En la clase de inglés tengo que leer un libro que es muy aburrido.

97. Comparisons

1 (a) Mi madre es **más alta que** mi padre.
  (b) Luisa es **menos seria que** Marcos.
  (c) Este autobús es **más lento que** el tren.
  (d) La fruta es **tan sana / saludable como** las verduras.
  (e) Esta camisa es **tan cara como** aquella chaqueta.
2 (a) el mejor (b) los peores (c) la más pequeña / baja
  (d) las más difíciles (e) las menos aburridas
3 (a) Mi primo/a es más fuerte que tu tío.
  (b) Su móvil es pequeñísimo.
  (c) El examen de español es facilísimo.
  (d) Las películas de aventura son tan emocionantes como las películas de acción.
  (e) Mi instituto es el más viejo / antiguo.
  (f) Las ciencias son menos aburridas que las matemáticas.
  (g) Mi amigo Omar es nuestro mejor jugador.

98. Other adjectives

1

Masc. sing.	Fem. sing.	Masc. plural	Fem. plural
este	esta	estos	estas
ese	esa	esos	esas
aquel	**aquella**	**aquellos**	**aquellas**

2   (a) estas chaquetas   (b) esta camiseta   (c) aquella chica
    (d) esos huevos   (e) ese móvil   (f) aquellas revistas
    (g) este libro   (h) esa película   (i) aquel tren   (j) estos sombreros   (k) esas naranjas   (l) aquellos chicos
3   (a) cada   (b) misma   (c) algunas   (d) todos   (e) otra
4   (a) Todos   (b) Algunos   (c) Todos   (d) algunos   (e) misma
    (f) mismos

99. Pronouns

1

yo	I
tú	you singular
él	he
ella	**she**
nosotros	we (masc.)
nosotras	**we (fem.)**
vosotros	**you plural (masc.)**
vosotras	you plural (fem.)
ellos	**they (masc.)**
ellas	they (fem.)

2   (a) Las hemos perdido.   (b) La han perdido.
    (c) Carmen lo come.   (d) Lo compro.   (e) No la bebo.
    (f) No la lavo.   (g) Lo quiero escribir. / Quiero escribirlo.
    (h) No quiero leerla. / No la quiero leer.   (i) La necesito ahora.
    (j) Vamos a venderla. / La vamos a vender.
3   (a) I am going to write to him / her this afternoon.
    (b) I visited them yesterday.
    (c) I will do it if I have time.
    (d) I gave him / her a present for his / her birthday.
    (e) Have you seen them?
    (f) Vino a visitarme a casa. / Me vino a visitar a casa.
    (g) Me mandaron la información.
    (h) Voy a comprarlos en línea. / Los voy a comprar en línea.

100. The present tense
1   (a) vivimos   (b) bailan   (c) vendo   (d) lleváis   (e) odias
    (f) come   (g) salimos   (h) escucha
2   (a) comen   (b) vivimos   (c) tienes   (d) hablan   (e) debe
    (f) grita   (g) chateo   (h) lee   (i) piensa   (j) Podéis
3   (a) cenamos   (b) trabajan   (c) tomo   (d) pone
    (e) compramos   (f) cuestan   (g) Quiero   (h) piden

101. Reflexive verbs
1

me	levanto		me	divierto
te	levantas		te	diviertes
se	levanta		se	divierte
nos	levantamos		nos	divertimos
os	levantáis		os	diviertís
se	levantan		se	divierten

2   (a) se   (b) se   (c) te   (d) se   (e) se   (f) Nos   (g) os   (h) Te
3   Todos los días Olivia **se levanta** temprano para ir a trabajar. **Trabaja** en una tienda de ropa famosa. Primero **se lava** los dientes y luego **se baña** y **se viste**. **Baja** las escaleras y **toma** el desayuno. Siempre **se sienta** en la cocina para comer. Después, **se lava** la cara en el cuarto de baño que está abajo, al lado de la cocina. **Se pone** la chaqueta y **sale** a las ocho y media porque el autobús llega a las nueve menos cuarto. **Vuelve** a casa a las siete de la tarde.

102. Irregular verbs (present)
1   (a) Yo no tengo la llave. ¿La tienes tú?
    (b) Paula le da flores a nuestra madre y yo le doy chocolates.
    (c) Cuando mi padre oye mi música, sale de la habitación rápidamente.
    (d) Si hace buen tiempo, yo no cojo el autobús.
    (e) Alba, cuando tú y Marcos venís a casa, siempre traéis regalos.

2   (a) oye   (b) conozco   (c) vienen   (d) cojo   (e) vamos   (f) sé
    (g) tienes   (h) pongo   (i) traigo   (j) dicen
3   (a) Voy a España.   (b) Tiene dos hermanas.
    (c) Oigo música.   (d) Dice la verdad.
    (e) Cogemos el autobús.   (f) Hacen los deberes.
    (g) Sales los sábados.   (h) Doy clases.   (i) Trae pan.
    (j) Pongo la fruta en la mesa.

103. *Ser* and *estar*
1   (a) está   (b) son   (c) Soy   (d) es   (e) Son   (f) está   (g) Estáis
    (h) Estamos
2   (a) Where is the bank? ('estar' for location)
    (b) My grandmothers are very nice. ('ser' for characteristics)
    (c) I am from Madrid but I work in Barcelona. ('ser' for where you are from)
    (d) The dress is green with white flowers. ('ser' for colours)
    (e) It's four thirty in the afternoon. ('ser' for time)
    (f) The wardrobe is next to the door. ('estar' for location)
    (g) You are (all) very sad today because the holidays have finished. ('estar' for moods)
    (h) We are ready for the history exam. ('estar' meaning 'ready' not 'clever')
3   (a), (d), (e), ✓
    (b) Mi amigo es alto y tiene el pelo negro.
    (c) Me duele la cabeza y estoy enfermo.
    (f) Mi madre es médica y mi padre es escritor.

104. The gerund / present participle
1   (a) comiendo – eating
    (b) estudiando – studying
    (c) corriendo – running
    (d) tomando – taking (drinking / eating)
    (e) diciendo – saying
    (f) recibiendo – receiving
    (g) escribiendo – writing
    (h) escuchando – listening
    (i) aprendiendo – learning
    (j) viendo – seeing
2   (a) Estoy escuchando música.
    (b) Están navegando por Internet.
    (c) Estamos viendo una película.
    (d) Estás hablando con amigos.
3   (a) Estaba jugando al baloncesto cuando se rompió el dedo.
    (b) Estaban comiendo cuando su madre les llamó.
    (c) Estábamos tomando el sol cuando empezó a llover.
    (d) Estabas cantando cuando salió el tren.
    (e) Estábamos viendo la tele cuando nuestro hermanastro volvió a casa.
    (f) Estaba jugando al tenis cuando llamó.
    (g) Estabais escuchando al profesor cuando entró la directora.
    (h) Estaba estudiando en la biblioteca cuando oyó el ruido.

105. The preterite tense
1   (a) sacaron   (b) volvimos   (c) compró   (d) llegaste
    (e) trabajasteis   (f) fue   (g) di   (h) tuvimos   (i) pidieron
    (j) leyó
2   (a) fui   (b) tuvimos   (c) dieron   (d) fue   (e) dio, pagué
    (f) fueron   (g) dijo   (h) fue   (i) Hice   (j) tuve
3   **Fui** al cine con mis amigos y **vimos** una película de acción. Después **comimos** en un restaurante. **Comí** una hamburguesa con jamón y queso, y mi amiga Lola **comió** pescado con patatas. **Bebimos** zumo de manzana y mi amigo Tom **comió** un pastel de chocolate pero yo no **comí** postre. Después del restaurante **fui** en tren a casa de mi prima. El viaje **fue** largo y aburrido. **Volví** a casa y **me acosté** a las once de la noche.

106. The imperfect tense
1   (b) De pequeños, íbamos a la costa todos los veranos. ✓
    (c) Había mucha gente en el museo y los cuadros eran muy bonitos. ✓
    (e) Cuando eran más jóvenes, no comían fruta ni verdura.

(h) <u>Estaba</u> nervioso cada vez que <u>hacía</u> una prueba de matemáticas. ✓
(j) <u>Nevaba</u> todos los días y <u>hacía</u> un frío terrible. ✓

2 (a) On Wednesday we went to the park and we played tennis for an hour and a half. (preterite for completed action in the past)
(b) When we were little, we used to go to the coast every summer. (imperfect for 'used to')
(c) There were a lot of people in the museum and the pictures were really lovely. (imperfect for descriptions)
(d) My father prepared a vegetarian meal for us. (preterite for a completed action in the past)
(e) When they were younger, they didn't eat either fruit or vegetables. (imperfect to describe repeated actions in the past)
(f) Gabriela arrived in Madrid by train to start her new job. (preterite for completed action in the past)
(g) Yesterday we met in the café and we talked all afternoon. (preterite for completed action in the past)
(h) I used to be nervous every time I did a Maths test. (imperfect for 'used to')
(i) I had a very good time because it was sunny and it didn't rain. (preterite for completed action in the past)
(j) It snowed every day and it was terribly cold. (imperfect for descriptions)

3 (a) tenía (b) vivía (c) estaba (d) lavé (e) trabajaban
   (f) gastó (g) comíamos (h) jugué

107. The future tense
1 (a) jugar (b) Va (c) a (d) voy (e) Vas (f) Vais (g) va (h) ir (i) vamos (j) Voy
2 (a) Vamos a ver la película. (b) No trabajaré los lunes.
   (c) Van a coger el metro. (d) Irá al Reino Unido.
   (e) Van a jugar con mi hermano. (f) Irás a España.
3 (a) va a ir (b) voy a ir (c) voy a pasar (d) voy a vivir
   (e) voy a viajar (f) vamos a visitar (g) vamos a probar
   (h) Va a ser

108. The conditional tense
1 (a) compraríamos – we would buy
   (b) saldrían – they would go out
   (c) trabajaríais – you (all) would work
   (d) estaría – he / she / it would be
   (e) jugarías – you (sing.) would play
   (f) vendríamos – we would come
   (g) podrías – you (sing.) could
   (h) habría – there would be
2 (a) iría (b) tomarían (c) trabajaría (d) ganaríamos
   (e) habría (f) usaría (g) tendría (h) lucharían
   (i) ganaría (j) compartiríamos
3 NB All answers can use either *podrías* or *deberías*.
   (a) Podrías leer para relajarte.
   (b) Podrías comer más frutas y verduras.
   (c) Deberías hacer más ejercicio.
   (d) Deberías ir al médico.
   (e) Deberías acostarte temprano.
   (f) Podrías ir al dentista.

109. The perfect tense
1

	haber	+ past participle
yo	he	hablado comido vivido
tú	has	
él / ella / usted	ha	
nosotros / nosotras	hemos	
vosotros / vosotras	habéis	
ellos / ellas / ustedes	han	

2

Infinitive	Irregular past participle	Scrambled version
hacer	hecho	beatiro (abierto)
volver	vuelto	cheoh (hecho)
abrir	abierto	cidoh (dicho)
romper	roto	lutove (vuelto)
ver	visto	sotupe (puesto)
escribir	escrito	tisvo (visto)
poner	puesto	toro (roto)
decir	dicho	triseco (escrito)

3 (a) We have lost our car.
   (b) Have you studied Spanish?
   (c) They have bought a laptop.
   (d) I have done my homework.
   (e) We have seen a very informative programme.
   (f) Me he roto el brazo.
   (g) Han perdido sus llaves.
   (h) Hemos bebido mucho té.
   (i) ¿Has visitado el museo hoy?
   (j) Los profesores han abierto las ventanas.

110. Giving instructions
1 (a) Sube a la derecha. (b) Cruza la plaza.
   (c) Di tu nombre. (d) Ten cuidado. (e) Ven aquí.
   (f) Canta más bajo. (g) Lee en voz alta. (h) Escucha bien.
   (i) Bebe el agua. (j) Haz este ejercicio.
2 (a) Subid a la derecha. (b) Cruzad la plaza.
   (c) Pasad la biblioteca. (d) Tened cuidado. (e) Venid aquí.
   (f) Cantad más bajo. (g) Leed en voz alta.
   (h) Escuchad bien. (i) Bebed el agua. (j) Haced este ejercicio.
3

tú commands	*vosotros/as* commands
(a) Baja la música. (b) Haz la cama. (c) Visita el museo. (d) Canta con la música.	(a) Comprad las verduras en el mercado. (b) Escoged vuestros cuartos / vuestras habitaciones. (c) Discutid el problema primero. (d) Reciclad esas botellas.

111. The present subjunctive
1 (a) haga (b) tengas (c) venga (d) sea (e) vayas (f) tenga (g) sea (h) vaya (i) haga (j) vengas
2 (a) vayas (b) hagas (c) seas (d) venga (e) tenga (f) tengas (g) haga (h) tenga
3 (a) Mi hermana quiere que haga un pastel.
   (b) Me molesta que no vengas conmigo.
   (c) Espero que tengas suerte con los exámenes.
   (d) Cuando vayas a España, debes visitar Barcelona.
   (e) Puedes ir a las Islas Canarias cuando seas mayor.

112. Negatives
1 (a) No estudio geografía.
   (b) No vamos a la ciudad.
   (c) Ricardo no compró una bicicleta nueva.
   (d) Sus padres no vieron la tele.
   (e) No voy a ir a España la semana próxima.
2 1 H 2 E 3 A 4 B 5 G 6 C 7 D 8 F
3 (a) Mis profesores nunca gritan si hago una pregunta.
   (b) No como nada durante el descanso.
   (c) En mi familia nunca tuvimos un perro.
   (d) Aquí no tengo ni vestidos, ni faldas, ni camisetas.
   (e) No vas a comprar ningún coche.
   (f) Mis padres no escuchan a nadie.
4 (a) Por la tarde nunca bebemos / tomamos café.
   (b) No canto ni bailo ni toco (ningún) instrumento musical.
   (c) No hablan ningún idioma.
   (d) No podemos hablar con nadie durante el examen.
   (e) Nunca fumaré porque es malo para la salud.

113. Special verbs

1

me		I like
te		you like
le	gusta (sing.)	he / she / it likes
nos	gustan (plural)	we like
os		you (all) like
les		they like

2 (a) A Paula le gusta … (b) ¿Te gustan …
(c) Nos interesa … (d) A Manuel le duele …
(e) Le encanta … (f) No … me importa …
(g) Me hace falta … (h) Le falta …

3 (a) Acabo de ver una película muy buena / buenísima.
(b) Lleva dos horas trabajando en el jardín.
(c) Nadim acaba de terminar su carrera universitaria / en la universidad.
(d) Llevamos un mes viviendo aquí.
(e) Tus abuelos acaban de salir.
(f) Llevo tres años estudiando español.

114. *Por* and *para*

1 (a) For my birthday I want a new mobile phone.
(b) My friend works for an international company.
(c) Apps for the iPhone are incredible.
(d) I eat a lot of vegetables and fish in order to keep fit.
(e) You need the key to get into the house.
(f) Smoking is very bad for your health.

2 (a) El coche rojo pasó por las calles antiguas.
(b) Normalmente por la mañana me gusta tomar huevos con pan.
(c) Mandé la información por correo electrónico.
(d) Me gustaría cambiar este jersey por otro.
(e) En la tienda ganamos quince euros por hora.

3 (a) Para (b) para (c) por (d) para

115. Asking questions

1 Why? – ¿Por qué? What? – ¿Qué?
When? – ¿Cuándo? How? – ¿Cómo?
Where? – ¿Dónde? Where to? – ¿Adónde?
Which? – ¿Cuál? Which ones? – ¿Cuáles?
How much? – ¿Cuánto/a? How many? – ¿Cuántos/as?

2 (a) Dónde (b) Cuándo (c) Cuáles (d) Cuánto
(e) Qué (f) Cómo (g) Adónde (h) Cuántas

3 1D, 2G, 3A, 4H, 5B, 6C, 7E, 8F

116. The passive

1 (a) fue escrita (b) serán construidos (c) es usado
(d) son limpiadas (e) fueron presentados
(f) fue reconocida (g) son aceptados (h) fueron mandados

2 (a) The novel was written last century.
(b) The flats will be built next year.
(c) The sports centre is used by thousands of people every week.
(d) The facilities are cleaned every day.
(e) This morning the students were presented / introduced to the head teacher / principal.
(f) Last night the actress was recognised several times in the restaurant.
(g) Normally (the) tourists are accepted on the islands.
(h) Due to the snow yesterday, the children were sent home.

3 (a) Se publicarán (b) Se mandarán (c) se basa
(d) Se organiza (e) Se limpió (f) Se robaron

117. Numbers

1 (a) veinte 20 (b) cuarenta y ocho 48
(c) nueve 9 (d) cien 100 (e) catorce 14
(f) mil 1,000 (g) trescientos 300 (h) cincuenta y siete 57
(i) veintitrés 23 (j) quince 15 (k) diecinueve 19
(l) quinientos 500 (m) un millón 1,000,000
(n) novecientos 900 (o) ochenta y ocho 88
(p) setenta y seis 76 (q) sesenta y siete 67 (r) diez 10
(s) cero 0 (t) veintinueve 29

2 (a) mil novecientos noventa y nueve
(b) el diez de octubre
(c) el primero / uno de enero
(d) el tres de marzo
(e) dos mil trece
(f) el dieciséis de noviembre
(g) el treinta de mayo
(h) mil novecientos sesenta y ocho
(i) dos mil dos
(j) el veintiuno de abril

3 (a) Son las siete y cuarto. (b) Es la una y veinticinco.
(c) Son las nueve menos veinticinco. (d) Son las once y diez.
(e) Son las cuatro menos cuarto. (f) Son las diez menos diez.
(g) Son las cinco y media. (h) Son las doce.

118. Paper 1: Speaking (Foundation)

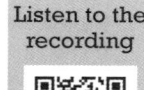

Listen to the recording

1 Sample answers to follow-on questions:
(a) Me gusta ir al cine y jugar al baloncesto.
(b) Soy un buen amigo. Escucho y ayudo a mis amigos.

Listen to the recording

2 Sample answers:
T: Buenos días. ¿Cómo puedo ayudarle?
S: Quiero ir a la costa.
T: Muy bien. ¿Qué día?
S: Para el domingo, por favor.
T: ¿Para cuántas personas?
S: Para cuatro personas.
T: Vale. ¿Qué tal las vacaciones?
S: Las vacaciones son excelentes.
T: Muy bien. ¿Tiene una pregunta?
S: ¿A qué hora sale el autobús?
T: Sale a las nueve.

3 Sample answer:

Picture 1
En la foto hay un grupo de estudiantes. Todos llevan una camisa blanca y una corbata porque es su uniforme escolar. Los chicos no están hablando, están pensando y escribiendo porque están haciendo un examen en el colegio. Están en una clase con sillas y mesas en fila. Están muy serios porque es un examen importante.

Listen to the recording

Sample answers to follow-on questions:
(a) Mi uniforme no es cómodo y no me gusta nada. Llevamos una falda o pantalones grises, una camisa blanca y una chaqueta azul.
(b) Algunos exámenes no están mal, pero los exámenes de unas asignaturas son muy difíciles.

Picture 2
En la foto hay cuatro estudiantes y el profesor en una clase en el instituto. Los dos chicos tienen papel y bolígrafos y están discutiendo un proyecto. Las dos chicas están haciendo algo en el portátil y el profesor está ayudando. Todos están contentos y están interesados en la clase.

Listen to the recording

Sample answers to follow-on questions:
(a) Empezamos a las ocho y media y hay tres clases antes del descanso. Luego, hay dos más y la hora de comer a las doce y media. Terminamos a las tres y media.
(b) Me gustan las actividades en grupo porque es divertido trabajar con mis amigos y los otros estudiantes.

Sample answers to broader thematic context questions:
T: ¿Cuál es tu asignatura favorita?
S: Mi asignatura favorita es la religión. Es muy interesante aprender sobre las ideas de la gente en otros países y de otras religiones. También, la profesora es muy simpática y trabajadora. Prepara clases muy buenas.

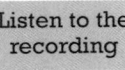

T: ¿Qué haces durante el descanso en el instituto?
S: Normalmente, como un bocadillo y hablo con mis amigos y amigas. Tenemos que salir al patio si hace buen tiempo, pero si llueve nos quedamos en la clase.
T: ¿Cuándo haces los deberes?
S: Intento hacer mis deberes cuando llego a casa después de las clases, pero muchas veces los dejo hasta las siete, después de la cena. No me gusta hacerlos muy tarde.
T: ¿Qué hiciste en tu última clase de español?
S: Hice un ejercicio de escuchar, y trabajé con un compañero leyendo textos en voz alta para practicar para el examen de hoy.
T: ¿Con qué asignaturas piensas continuar en el futuro?
S: Espero continuar con inglés, historia y religión, o español, pero depende de mis notas.
T: ¿Qué es lo bueno de tu instituto?
S: Mi instituto es grande y moderno y tiene una biblioteca nueva. Tenemos profesores muy buenos.
T: ¿Qué parte de tu instituto te gustaría cambiar?
S: Primero, creo que necesitamos más ordenadores. Los ordenadores que tenemos son viejos y no hay suficientes. También me encantaría tener una piscina.
T: ¿Qué piensas de las reglas del instituto?
S: Creo que las reglas son necesarias. Pero pienso que el uniforme no es importante.
T: ¿Vas a ir a la universidad?
S: En este momento no sé. Voy a continuar con mis estudios de las asignaturas que me gustan más, y durante los dos años del curso, voy a pensar en mis opciones para el futuro.
T: ¿Qué tipo de trabajo te gustaría tener en el futuro?
S: Me gusta mucho escribir y creo que me gustaría trabajar para un periódico o una revista. Sería ideal trabajar en casa, pero no me importaría trabajar en una oficina.

119. Paper 2: Listening (Foundation)
1. (a) B (b) A (c) C
2. B, C, E
3. (a) train (b) bus (c) dangerous
4. A, D, E
5. (a) B (b) C (c) A (d) C
6. (a) too much sun / sunbathing
   (b) (try to) sleep
   (c) not sunbathe / keep out of the sun
7. (a) B (b) C (c) A
8. (a) sea (b) old town (c) rents a flat (d) in the pool
   (e) reading
9. B, E, F
10. (a) B (b) A (c) B (d) C
11. (a) (i) (which is) the best university in the area
       (ii) very high grades / marks
    (b) (i) Carla
       likes: the new science teacher
       dislikes: not being able to carry on with cooking (classes)
       (ii) Alejandro
       likes: being able to play / playing computer games during lunch
       dislikes: that he has lost his Maths (exercise) book
12. 1 Nuestra **prima** tiene dos **hijos**.
    2 Mi **hermano** no tiene mucha **confianza**.
    3 Me **llevo** bien con mis **parientes**.
    4 Todos tenemos los ojos marrones.
    5 Yo tengo el pelo rubio.
    6 Los viernes me gusta cocinar.

122. Paper 3: Reading (Foundation)
1. (a) Sara (b) Toni (c) Emilio (d) Emilio (e) Toni (f) Sara
2. A, D, F
3. (a) (i) B (ii) A (b) B
4. (a) One opinion of the director's last film: very slow / hard to understand
   What film is on the other screen: a love story
   (b) One reason the cinema is noisy: people eating / people talking
   Why he prefers to watch at home: He can stop the film (when he wants).
5. B, E, F
6. (a) three months (b) Art (c) Science
7. (a) (i) C (ii) B (iii) A (iv) C
7. (b) B
8. (a) (i) market (ii) eat something (iii) compare prices
8. (b) (i) A (ii) B
8. (c) (i) the amount of salt in food / the amount of sugar in food
   (ii) buy natural ingredients
9. (a) Reason she likes the centre: It has swimming lessons for disabled people.
   The one problem with it: not much room for parking / not much room for cars
   (b) Reason he likes the bar: It has a view of the pool. / He can watch his children in the pool (from there).
   What he recommends: raising the water temperature / making the water a bit warmer
   (c) What she did this week: went to her first (modern) dance class
   What she would change: She wants the classes to start earlier.
10. (a) I hope to continue / carry on with my studies.
    (b) I want a job during / for the summer holidays.
    (c) We had a party after the exams.
    (d) My cousin is studying abroad for a year.
    (e) I would like to learn to play a musical instrument.

127. Paper 4: Writing (Foundation)
1. Sample answers:
   1 Es una playa muy grande.
   2 Los hoteles son muy altos.
   3 Hace mucho sol.
   4 Unos hombres juegan al vóleibol.
2. (a) Sample answer:
Hago ejercicio cuatro veces por semana. Voy al instituto a pie y voy a la piscina los domingos. También como mucha fruta y verduras.
Creo que la comida rápida no es muy sana porque tiene mucha grasa.
Mañana voy a jugar al tenis con mi amigo.
2. (b) Sample answer:
Mi película favorita es un musical y la música es excelente. Tiene momentos muy divertidos, pero a veces es triste también.
Me gusta ver programas de deporte en la televisión, como partidos de fútbol, pero otros son aburridos.
Voy a ir al cine con mis amigos el viernes.
3. (a) Sample answer:
Durante las vacaciones de verano es importante descansar y dormir porque ir al instituto es mucho trabajo.
Odio tener deberes en verano porque quiero pasarlo bien y divertirme. No quiero estudiar más. Pero los profesores nos dan deberes todo el tiempo.
El invierno pasado, hizo mucho frío y llovió. Me quedé en casa y jugué con mi videoconsola o leí un libro. También vi unas series en Netflix.
En el futuro quiero viajar a muchos países diferentes y me gustaría ir con un amigo o un grupo de amigos.

3 (b) Sample answer:
Normalmente, tomo el desayuno a las ocho, la comida a la una y la cena a las seis.
Creo que la comida española es muy rica. Me encanta la paella y me gustan mucho las tapas. Pero creo que los postres son un poco aburridos.
La semana pasada cociné una tortilla de queso con patatas fritas para la familia. También preparé bocadillos para llevar al instituto para mi almuerzo.
Para el cumpleaños de mi padre, la semana que viene, vamos a salir a comer a un restaurante argentino.

4 (a) Tengo dieciséis años y soy alto/a.
(b) Mi cumpleaños es el dos de julio.
(c) Mi casa no está lejos de la ciudad / del pueblo.
(d) Normalmente me levanto a las siete y media de la mañana.
(e) Ayer hice un pastel para mi abuela.

129. Paper 1: Speaking (Higher)

1 Read aloud
Sample answers to follow-on questions:
(a) Para mí, es mandar mensajes.
(b) No, solo cuando van al instituto.

2 Role play
T: Buenos días. ¿Cómo puedo ayudarle?
S: ¿Tiene habitaciones libres?
T: ¿Qué tipo de habitaciones quiere?
S: Quiero dos habitaciones dobles, por favor.
T: ¿Para cuántas noches?
S: Vamos a estar aquí tres noches.
T: Muy bien. ¿Qué piensa de nuestra región?
S: Es una región muy bonita y hace muy buen tiempo.
T: Vale. ¿Tiene una pregunta?
S: ¿A qué hora son las comidas en el hotel?
T: Aquí tiene la información.

3 Picture-based task
Picture 1
Sample answer:
En la foto hay un hombre y una mujer y están en el campo. Es una zona muy verde con campos y un bonito río con agua fría y limpia. Es verano y hay muchas hojas en los árboles. Hace buen tiempo y bastante calor porque la mujer lleva una camiseta rosa y el hombre lleva pantalones cortos. Les gusta estar en la naturaleza y están mirando los pájaros. Creo que van a hacer camping porque llevan mucho equipo.

Sample answers to follow-on questions for Picture 1
(a) El pueblo donde vivo no es muy bonito, pero la gente es muy simpática. Estamos cerca de zonas hermosas y de dos grandes ciudades.
(b) Me gusta más vivir en la ciudad porque hay más que hacer. Hay centros de deporte, cines y restaurantes y puedes salir al campo de vez en cuando si quieres pasar un día tranquilo.

Picture 2
Sample answer:
La foto es del centro de una ciudad grande y moderna. Hay muchos edificios altos de pisos y oficinas. Las carreteras son amplias y hay muchos coches. Una chica está en primer plano; es una chica bonita con el pelo largo y negro. Lleva una chaqueta color naranja y parece feliz porque está sonriendo. Está levantando la mano para parar el autobús o para decir hola a un amigo en la calle.

Sample answers to follow-on questions for Picture 2
(a) Creo que en la ciudad, siempre hay ruido porque hay muchas personas, mucho tráfico y parece que siempre hay construcción.

(b) Creo que es bastante bueno por lo general.
Sample answers to broader thematic context questions:
T: ¿Cómo sería tu casa ideal?
S: La casa de mis sueños sería un piso grande y moderno en el último piso de un edificio en el centro de la ciudad. Tendría ventanas muy grandes con vistas de toda la ciudad. Habría mucha tecnología con controles electrónicos, y podría encender y apagar las luces, la televisión y la música con solo mi voz.
T; ¿Cuál es el problema del medio ambiente más serio en tu región?
S: Sin duda, es la basura. Las calles y el parque siempre están muy sucios porque la gente tira papeles y botellas de plástico por todas partes. No debería ser necesario, pero creo que el ayuntamiento debería gastar más dinero en limpiar las zonas públicas del pueblo.
T: ¿Qué hacen los turistas cuando vienen a tu región?
S: Pues los turistas no vienen a mi pueblo porque no hay nada que ver, pero van a las dos ciudades grandes y a la región de lagos al norte de donde vivo. Hay mucha cultura en las ciudades como estadios, salas de conciertos, museos y teatros.
T: ¿Dónde recomiendas ir a comer en tu zona?
S: Tenemos un nuevo restaurante de tapas que acaba de abrir. Todavía no he ido, pero mis amigos dicen que es excelente. Los dueños son de Barcelona.
T: ¿Qué espacios verdes hay en tu pueblo o ciudad?
S: Hay dos parques grandes. Uno está lleno de flores y árboles y está bien si quieres pasear con el perro o sentarte al sol. El otro tiene un parque infantil y zonas para jugar al baloncesto y al tenis.
T: ¿Qué hiciste la última vez que fuiste a la ciudad con tus amigos?
S: Fuimos a un gran centro de juegos. Tiene muchos juegos electrónicos, y videoconsolas, pero también actividades más activas como el tenis de mesa. Además, está cerca de un gran centro comercial con un montón de restaurantes y fuimos a comer allí después.
T: ¿Cómo es el clima en tu región?
S: Es muy malo. Los inviernos son muy duros porque el cielo está gris todo el tiempo y llueve mucho. Casi no se ve el sol. En verano tenemos un tiempo un poco mejor, pero me gustaría tener más días de calor.
T: ¿Dónde te gustaría vivir en el futuro?
S: Creo que me gustaría quedarme en mi país, pero también me encantaría vivir al lado del mar. Sería guay pasear en la playa, aun en invierno.
T: ¿Cómo era tu región en el pasado?
S: Era una zona con mucha industria, y como consecuencia había bastante polución. La gente trabajaba a menudo en tareas sucias y a veces peligrosas, y su salud sufría. Es mucho mejor ahora.
T: ¿Qué cambiarías en tu pueblo o ciudad?
S: Necesitamos un centro de deportes con actividades para gente de todas las edades. En el pueblo no hay mucho que hacer, y sería muy bueno tener una piscina, campos de fútbol para alquilar, y clases de vóleibol, por ejemplo.

131. Paper 2: Listening (Higher)

1 (a) B (b) C (c) A
2 (a) sea (b) old town (c) rents a flat (d) in the pool (e) reading
3 B, E, F
4 (a) B (b) A (c) B (d) C
5 (a) to pay his phone bill
(b) she is saving for her holidays
(c) he would have to work late hours (in the week)
6 (a) hottest (b) cloud, rain

7   (a) Amira
    Advantage: keeps your options open
    Disadvantage: still have to do P.E.
    (b) Vicente
    Advantage: it prepares you for university
    Disadvantage: you still have the same teachers
    (c) Marta
    Advantage: being with her old classmates / not going somewhere new where she doesn't know anyone
    Disadvantage: school is far from home / her house
8   (a) (i) C   (ii) B   (iii) C
    (b) (i) B   (ii) A   (iii) B
9   (a) B, D, E
    (b) (i) give presentations to the students (ii) boss / manager of a (large) scientific firm / company (iii) how she got to (be in) such an important post / position (iv) the problems that people with disabilities have in the workplace
10 1 La **catedral** fue **construida** en el último **siglo**.
    2 El **barrio gótico** es muy **pintoresco**.
    3 Los edificios en el centro son antiguos.
    4 Hay que ver el paisaje.
    5 La feria empieza el domingo.
    6 Quiero seguir este camino por el bosque.

134. Paper 3: Reading (Higher)

1   (a) three months   (b) Art   (c) Science
2   (a) (i) C   (ii) B   (iii) A   (iv) C
    (b) B
3   (a) (i) market   (ii) eat something   (iii) compare prices
    (b) (i) A   (ii) B
    (c) (i) the amount of salt in food / the amount of sugar in food
        (ii) buy natural ingredients
4   (a) (i) very clear images / pictures / photos of the houses
        (ii) it doesn't show (exactly) where the houses are
    (b) B
5   (a) A, B, C
    (b) (i) some of the loveliest places in the area
        (ii) it was very hot / they couldn't open the windows
        (iii) they were crossing a border (between two countries)
        (iv) the passports were being checked
6   (a) B, C
    (b) (i) you get a discount of 2 euros / you pay 2 euros less to enter
        (ii) hot and cold meals / dishes
        (iii) climb trees
7   (a) (i) A   (ii) C   (iii) B
    (b) (i) the sons and daughters of very rich people
        (ii) she is the daughter of one of the cleaners
8   (a) that he didn't get the job
    (b) what he can do to improve for the future
    (c) he would have got on with the others (in the team)
    (d) he did not know much about the company / firm / he did not know much about the work they did / do
    (e) he asked about pay and holidays
9   I really like doing physical exercise and every day I go out running through the big park in the city. I often prepare vegetarian meals for the family. I also relax by listening to music. My brother is very like my father and they are both very keen on basketball. They went to see a match yesterday.

139. Paper 4: Writing (Higher)

1(a) Sample answer:
Durante las vacaciones de verano es importante descansar y dormir porque ir al instituto es mucho trabajo.
Odio tener deberes en verano porque quiero pasarlo bien y divertirme. No quiero estudiar más. Pero los profesores nos dan deberes todo el tiempo.
El invierno pasado, hizo mucho frío y llovió. Me quedé en casa y jugué con mi videoconsola o leí un libro. También vi unas series en Netflix.
En el futuro quiero viajar a muchos países diferentes y me gustaría ir con un amigo o un grupo de amigos.

1(b) Sample answer:
Normalmente, tomo el desayuno a las ocho, la comida a la una y la cena a las seis.
Creo que la comida española es muy rica. Me encanta la paella y me gustan mucho las tapas. Pero creo que los postres son un poco aburridos.
La semana pasada cociné una tortilla de queso con patatas fritas para la familia. También preparé bocadillos para llevar al instituto para mi almuerzo.
Para el cumpleaños de mi padre, la semana que viene, vamos a salir a comer a un restaurante argentino.

2(a) Sample answer:
Un buen amigo es una persona que se lleva bien contigo. Normalmente tienes mucho en común con un amigo y compartís intereses. Un buen amigo te escucha y siempre está ahí cuando necesitas hablar.
Cuando sales con un gran grupo de amigos puede ser muy divertido, pero es difícil hablar con todos y acabas ignorando a algunos.
El mes pasado fui con otros tres amigos a ver un concierto en un gran estadio en la ciudad. Era un concierto de uno de nuestros grupos favoritos. La música fue excelente, pero había miles de personas allí y no fue fácil ver al grupo.
Este fin de semana, mi familia y yo vamos a pasear en una zona muy bonita que está lejos de la ciudad. Tiene muchos campos y un río muy grande. Después comeremos en un restaurante; mi padre ya ha reservado la mesa.

2(b) Sample answer:
En el instituto, mi clase favorita es la clase de historia. La profesora diseña clases muy interesantes y hacemos una gran variedad de actividades. A veces vemos un vídeo, o leemos textos de siglos pasados, o tenemos un debate.
Si digo la verdad, las reglas del instituto tienen sentido porque simplemente tratan de respetar a las otras personas para sacar las mejores notas posibles en tus estudios. Sería útil usar el móvil en clase a veces, para cosas educativas, pero entiendo las razones por las que no está permitido.
Me gustó mi primer día en la escuela. Tenía ganas de ir y no tenía miedo. Lo pasé muy bien.
Creo que todos los estudiantes deberían estudiar cosas prácticas para el futuro, por ejemplo, cómo ahorrar tu dinero y los tipos de cuentas de banco que hay. También algo muy importante es estudiar más sobre el medio ambiente.

3   Cada año / Todos los años voy a un pequeño pueblo / una pequeña ciudad en la costa en el este de España.
    Hay muchos turistas allí y el ambiente es muy agradable.
    Normalmente hace mucho calor y sol, especialmente por la tarde.
    Sin embargo, en agosto pasado tuvimos dos días de lluvia / llovió dos días. Volveremos / Vamos a volver este verano también.